TELEVISION AND
LANGUAGE SKILLS

Television
and Language Skills

Richard Sherrington

LONDON
OXFORD UNIVERSITY PRESS
1973

Oxford University Press, Ely House, London W1

GLASGOW NEW YORK TORONTO MELBOURNE WELLINGTON
CAPE TOWN IBADAN NAIROBI DAR ES SALAAM LUSAKA ADDIS ABABA
DELHI BOMBAY CALCUTTA MADRAS KARACHI LAHORE DACCA
KUALA LUMPUR SINGAPORE HONG KONG TOKYO

ISBN 0 19 437005 4

© Oxford University Press 1973

Printed in Great Britain by
Western Printing Services Ltd
Bristol

Contents

Preface

Who is this book for? Specifically, it is for those people who are concerned with the use of television in teaching language skills. Ten years ago, that group of people would have included companies making language-teaching films for world-wide sale; a few TV stations with an educational component; and hard-pressed teachers in those countries where the films and TV programmes were adopted for classroom use.

Since that time, the importance of television in education has grown; the importance of learning foreign languages has grown. Most significant, all the varied means which have been developed for teaching languages have been strengthened by being used in combinations: tape-slide courses, radiovision courses, textbook and television courses, packaged record and textbook courses; and a growing number of teachers wish to make use of all these techniques—and also retain their professional independence. The question no longer is: 'We have a textbook, or a television series, or a language laboratory; now what are we going to do with it?' Rather the question is: 'This is our teaching problem: what is the best combination of means with which to solve it?' The question has political, social and economic ramifications. It involves policy makers, curriculum planners, educational research teams; it involves headmasters, inspectors, department heads, teacher-trainers and the teaching body itself; it involves the textbook writers, the manufacturers of audio-visual aids; and it involves the broadcasting administration, the scriptwriters, producers, directors, presenters, set designers, film men and graphics artists.

Each of these elements in the total teaching scheme can only operate efficiently if it understands the central problem—what is to be taught—and the contribution which each element is making towards solving the problem. This means that each element has to know something of the disciplines and problems of the others:

the textbook writer of the TV producer, the set designer of the classroom teacher, the headmaster of the broadcasting administration. This book is one small contribution towards that mutual understanding.

The discipline of television and the discipline of language teaching has each developed a sense of its own unassailable professional respectability. When the two have met over the last ten years or so, one has always come badly out of the encounter, and that has always been language teaching. Television's professional ethic has been unconditionally accepted: that a series needs months, even years, to prepare; that too much teaching, too much practice, makes for boring viewing; that the standards of lighting, set design, sound quality and make-up must be of the highest taste. Television's standards of quality and sophistication remain the same, whether the programme is entertainment for peak viewing time, historical drama, or an on-syllabus educational broadcast for schools. And the 'linguistic advisers', the teachers and the viewing students have accepted that ethic. Consequently, they have regarded television as a fringe activity—simply a convenient means of 'showing language in situations'. Their own professionalism was demonstrated on what they considered to be home ground—linguistic theory, teaching method and textbook courses.

The time has come for a change. Each discipline needs to exercise far greater flexibility than hitherto. We need to consider their similarities rather than their differences. Both are media of communication; there is no conflict between the language content and the televised content—what we talk about and what we show. A maths or physics course will dictate subject-matter to the TV producer, but not so the language course. Combined, the two media form a powerful force for other social or educational ends. It has been rather the forms—the disciplines—of each which have been in conflict. Yet, paradoxically, it is the forms of each which are so similar. We perform thousands of language operations every day, of varying complexity, in a variety of skills, decoding and encoding written and spoken information at a remarkable rate. Language functions are eclectic, not neatly structured, and, as we hope to show, teaching methods should reflect this eclecticism. Television, similarly, is uniquely capable of processing quantities of disconnected information so as to provide insights by juxtaposition, to draw inferences and make implications which could only be achieved otherwise by lengthy explanation. Television's visual eclecticism makes it ideally suited to the processes of language and language teaching.

The need for these changes is pressing. Although this book takes its examples mainly from English language teaching, the issues it discusses apply equally to any language at any level of development. Illiteracy remains a major world problem—one which television is helping to overcome. The demand for foreign language tuition is increasing, and, as political conglomerates become larger and more numerous, the need for everybody to understand and speak several languages will be vital. Communication satellites may be the only way of bringing this about. Certainly the existing methods and means of teaching languages do not possess the required speed or accessibility.

Television itself needs to change. It aspires to the standards of film because it hopes for the permanence of celluloid. But television is a throw-away medium; its strength lies in its immediacy. Current demands for more participation in programming, for the democratization of television, are aimed at those lengthy considerations of 'professional standards' which construct a series of filters and obstacles between the viewer and what he wants to see. There is often no difference between television and edited film, and there should be. Educational television has accepted that there can be no participation without organized conditions at the receiving end of the communication, and a system for allowing feedback from viewer to television producer. This is particularly vital in language-teaching programmes. It is a lesson which other programmes, especially current-affairs programmes, may have to learn as community television develops, and national networks are called upon to reflect society more broadly. The other lesson to be learned from educational television is that 'professional standards of quality and sophistication' are far less important, in judging a programme, than the effectiveness of the communication and its relevance to the viewer.

The subject of this book has implications for a wide range of issues. For many, language learning is the key to social and economic advancement; television is the most powerful means of communication ever known. Yet this is intended as a practical book, and it originates in experience of practical problems in a number of situations. I am indebted to Simon Murison-Bowie, whose refreshing approach to language teaching and course construction lies behind many ideas in this book; to Ato Abdu Mozayen and the Mass Media Centre in Addis Ababa, where many of the problems were first explored; to the English production team of the Instructional Television Centre, Tel-Aviv, for valuable comments and suggestions; to Professor Peter Strevens for his most generous advice and wisdom in the writing of; and to Piers Pendred, John Gartley and many other colleagues for conversations, comments, discussions, arguments and useful abuse.

Richard Sherrington

RRATUM
xi, line 9   *After* 'the writing of' *insert* 'Chapter 3'

1 Education and Technology

How do we learn? If the answer to this question was simple, it would be a little easier to answer the question: how do we teach? The fact remains, however, that both questions are extremely complex. In this century, the pressures upon educational development have increased enormously; the world demands better education and more of it. Theory succeeds theory, method follows method, technique supplants technique, in the effort to satisfy the demand. Each method has its supporters, and often their arguments have convinced government and business to invest large sums in hardware, software, training programmes and materials. In the developing countries, in need of 'developed' expertise and aid donations for their educational programmes, the authorities have had to accept the methodology of the moment, with the personnel trained in its application and the materials and machinery developed for it. Having made the conceptual leap from a traditional to a modern teaching methodology, and having committed limited funds to it, it is often hard to find that your 'modern' methodology is only the 'latest' methodology, and that it is already going out of fashion. It is sometimes hard to accept that no one knows how we learn; consequently, a teaching theory, methodology and technique can only be based upon assumptions and experience. We can say where a particular method falls short, what in it seems to work well; and we can adjust our techniques accordingly. Such periodic reassessments are part of educational development, and, hopefully, they lead to improved teaching systems. We have to proceed cautiously, and hope that this guess is better than the last one, since the fundamental question—how we learn—remains unanswered.

This book looks at the methodology of one subject area—language teaching—and the application of one technique—television. In the last few years, the prevailing theory and methodology of teaching languages has been subject to a certain amount of reassessment. The proponents of the 'direct', 'oral', or 'contextual' method spent much time justifying their approach to language teaching over what was called the 'grammar-translation' method. Now, the Direct Methodists themselves are up for reappraisal; the underlying theory of language acquisition is seen to be inadequate and the method itself raises many practical problems in the classroom. With the theory and the method under scrutiny, it becomes necessary to look at the techniques associated with them. Television, like the wax recording or the language laboratory, was seen to have enormous potential for the teaching of languages. In particular, it was ideal for the current methodology—situational language teaching. For the first time, linguistic behaviour could be set in its total extra-linguistic context; students could observe language as it really occurs, instead of experiencing it through a series of artificially created examples. The question now arises: if the theory and the method are inadequate, what are the implications for the technique? Where does the method fall short? What in it works well? How should we adjust the technique accordingly? Does television still have anything to offer to the student of languages?

A Fragmented Learning Process

The present reassessment of language-teaching theory and method reflects a general dissatisfaction with the idea of education as a simple matter of inputs and outputs. The basic idea is that good education requires good organization. From the structured Socratic dialogue to the intricate assembly of a conversation between a student and his computer, the key was 'organization'. The educative process had to be broken down into components of a greater or lesser size, then assembled in a graded sequence for instructional purposes. One could then regulate what went in and monitor what came out. The early rationale of programmed learning techniques was based upon this process.

At the same time, it was realized that there were a number of variables in the learning process which could only be guessed at from observable behaviour. Attempts had to be made to allow for these variables—in some way to control the various environments within which the input-output learning process took place. There were questions of physical environment: was the student captive within an organized education system, or a voluntary student subject to domestic pressures? If in a system, what were its administrative features? What was the status of the teacher? Was he free to manipulate the given syllabus and materials? Then there were questions of the psychological distinctions of the individual learner, which might affect his performance in the learning process: age, intelligence, problems of motivation, possible physical handicaps. These features influence the pacing and intensity of any course of study. There were also variables intrinsic to the course of study itself. In language learning, it was necessary to specify whether the language was to be taught as a second language or a foreign language; whether literacy, or oracy, or both was to be aimed at; what specific difficulties were likely to arise as a result of a bilingual comparison of the mother-tongue of the student and the language to be learnt. And so on. The input-output model of education was far from simple, because the organization of the inputs depended upon a wide variety of assumptions about the learner himself and his environment.

The analysis of these variables has led to an even narrower specification of the components of the learning process. One could not teach 'science'; one had to teach a particular aspect of science at a particular level for a particular type of learner in a particular type of educational system. To teach 'language' was no longer sufficient; one had to teach English for immigrants, Italian for businessmen, English for airline pilots, French or German for tourists. The general language coursebook continues to be written and used; but in recent years, it has given way to coursebooks for specific language areas, specific professional requirements and specific linguistic needs. The single classroom textbook has given way to a whole collection of coursebooks, each dealing with a different language skill.

Thus, the structural breakdown of the subject-matter to be taught, plus the further breakdown of material according to the environment and nature of the learner, led to a fragmentation of the learning process. Education became a matter of micro-structural organization.

The Application of Technology

What were the implications of this approach to the learning process for the technology which was increasingly being called in to assist it? Educational technology requires precise organization, both in itself and for its efficient application within the education system. But could it be utilized effectively within a microstructural approach to learning? It was possible to make a film on one aspect of electrostatics or ray optics, aimed at a particular type of audience; to demonstrate on television modes of address used among one section of the English middle class, for the benefit of French tourists. But whereas cost-effectiveness arguments are rarely brought to bear upon the teacher, his textbook, or his blackboard and chalk, they are an ·inevitable concomitant of educational technology. Development and production costs in money, time and manpower have to be recouped; to achieve this, the widest possible distribution is required. For the hardware, this involves the adaptation of machines for the greatest possible application, in as many educational areas as possible. Nor is the software—the films, the soundtapes and videotapes, the slides, the programmes—sufficiently inexpensive to produce to support a microstructural approach to learning. Again, wide application and distribution are necessary to justify time and money expended.

The application of technology to a microstructural education system therefore produces tension. The system requires that the learning process be broken down into small and precise components; the technology demands a large audience in a wide variety of educational environments, and, preferably, a subject-matter of broad application. This tension may be seen in the use of broadcast media for the Open University. Here, highly specialized television programmes, aimed at perhaps a few thousand students actually taking the particular course, are broadcast on an open television network, available to millions of people. This has been justified by drawing attention to the 'spin-off' effect of such wide distribution—the hope that many non-student viewers will be encouraged to apply for a university course.[1] It is inevitable that consciousness of the vast potential audience affects programme content to some extent.

The tension between technology and the education system is

discussed in the UNESCO: IIEP study, *The New Media: Memo to Educational Planners*. The concept of 'critical mass' is employed to relate distribution to cost; planners are advised to concentrate their use of the media at significant 'change points' in their educational system. 'Herein lies the basic difference between an "enrichment" approach and more strategic and advantageous uses of the new educational media.'[2] Recognizing that tension exists, the authors recommend a cautious, limited application of technology, justifying the expense in terms of the importance which planners place in the 'change point' where it is applied.

The term 'enrichment' has thus become a stigma attached to educational technology applied to a broad subject area for wide distribution. The BBC programme only loosely related to a school syllabus; the centrally produced ELT film series intended for world-wide consumption; the 'historical background' filmstrip or slide series for a literature course: such products are characterized as 'general interest' material, of fringe value compared to the bulk of the teaching carried on in the classroom. This is the pull at one end of the tension—that of an education system demanding precise specification of learning objectives and environment, and often too pressed for time to incorporate 'general interest' material in its course construction.

The pull at the other end of the tension is demonstrated by Richard Hooper's argument against the 'threat of localism' in the use of educational TV in America.[3] Against the obvious advantages of being able to make local programmes for local problems aimed at a known audience, as many universities are doing, there has to be weighed the enormous waste of money that such a policy involves. When the system requires an ever-increasing quantity of educational resources, there is hardly any attempt made to exchange tapes or films, or to pool them into a common fund of materials. To the educational technologist, working in an inevitably expensive field, it seems an absurdity to plead the autonomy of the individual teacher in his classroom, or the parochial problems of one institution or area, when, with a little adjustment, the same resources could be put at the disposal of a far greater number of students.

The use of closed-circuit television systems for education was thought to be a way round the kind of objections which Hooper raised. The programmes could be more easily geared to the content and pacing of a local syllabus; a wide range of subjects and levels of difficulty could be covered by a multi-channel system; the problem of timetable differences between schools could be overcome by a sufficient number of repeat transmissions. Above all, the cost was far less than that of open-network broadcasting. And yet closed-circuit television has set up its own kind of tension. The cost differential itself is seen to be a disadvantage: the student compares the cheap product at school with the expensive product on his TV set at home. There is a limit to the airtime available, and there remains the constant problem of balancing a thin skate over the curriculum with depth coverage of only a few subjects, with repeats to be worked in somehow. From the educational point of view, the main discontent with CCTV focuses on its tendency to conform totally to the prevailing educational system, almost cancelling out the contribution which the medium itself can bring to the learning process. It is frequently employed, for example, to solve the problem of large student intakes. As a result, 'the lecture', says Hooper, 'as the staple medium of college communication could now be set fair, thanks to television, for another hundred years'. The broadcasters' view is that the medium is not being used to the full. Says John Scupham: 'To think of the educational powers and possibilities of broadcasting in terms of ordinary classroom practice is to ignore both the wealth of resources and the obvious limitations of the media. A broadcast can stimulate, but cannot itself undertake, the dialectics of the classroom.'[4] The technology should not lean over backwards to accommodate the problems of the classroom teacher. Some other compromise must be found.

It is instructive to look at the development of programmed instruction techniques in the light of this tension between technology and the education system. Based upon the same behaviourist principles behind the fragmentation of the education process, it would seem that programmed learning techniques would have flourished. They allow for an infinite variety of learning environments, and embody self-correcting and self-pacing procedures. In practice, however, new developments in the field have not led to that integration of learning method and technique which their supporters wished for. The extension of branching programmes has had the effect of artificially bolstering less able students; it has been found that the more branches a student takes, the lower his test scores tend to be. Group work has been found to be as effective as self-paced tuition. In fact, the very concept of programmed instruction has developed, 'to include any provision for student learning which is capable of empirical trial, testing and revision. This includes television and sound radio broadcasts, practical and laboratory work, and even such apparently unformalizable activities as teaching judgement and creativity.'[5]

The application of technology to a microstructural approach to education, therefore, has led to a mess. The pendulum has swung backwards and forwards. Compromises have been made and all of them unsatisfactory. Hardly anywhere is technology taken for granted in the classroom as is the blackboard and chalk. Hardly anywhere has the education system adapted itself to the demands of the new technology. 'Alone of almost all the areas of human endeavour, education has been singularly reluctant to keep pace with the development of technology, and singularly resistant to the radical notion that conventional educational means are insufficient, perhaps even incapable, of serving society's needs in the latter half of the twentieth century.'[6] Technology cannot be other than what it is—it is there to be used. The education system, however, can change. The continued use of technology has led to the demand for a re-ordering of educational thinking.

Such a demand often puts the technology in first place, insisting that the system should be organized around it. Jacques Ellul's eulogy to 'technique' applauds such an approach: 'Technique . . . clarifies, arranges and rationalizes; it does in the domain of the abstract what the machine did in the domain of labour. It is efficient and brings efficiency to everything.'[7] But even if we do not place our technology in the centre of the system, its demands should have equal place with those of other elements in the system. The use of technology has implications for curriculum development, course construction, teacher training, and even the design of the buildings which will house the technological component. And these elements, in turn, have implications for the type of technology employed. All elements in this 'systems approach' are interrelated at every stage, from planning to implementation. Such a scheme, however, depends upon a re-adjustment of existing theory and methodology in the education system.

Rethinking the Teaching Process

Whether as a result of the impact of educational technology, or simply coincidental with it, there has been a shift in ideas about the learning process, and about the necessity to fragment it according to subject areas, categories of student and learning environments. The shift is reflected in educational administration in recent years.[8] There has been a move away from the social labelling of children at 11-plus, and students cease to be classified according to age, intelligence or qualifications. Streaming in primary and secondary sectors is seen more and more to be un-desirable and unnecessary. Courses at the Open University are available to anyone, irrespective of age or previous education. Adjustments in administration involve adjustments among the other components in the system. Where categories of learner no longer exist, the fragmentation of a course for each category becomes unnecessary.

Course content can be seen to be undergoing changes at the same time as they are occurring in educational administration. The move is away from the traditional subject stratification and more towards generalized courses of study. Developments in curricula emphasize unifying principles and overlapping areas. As human knowledge increases and multiplies, the selection of information to communicate to young people becomes an absurd business. Rather, the content emphasizes man and his place in society, the individual and his potential. Questions of educating people for a slot in society, training for specific jobs, are best left for short, intensive courses at a later stage.

The first prospectus of the Open University demonstrates how far it has accepted this shift in ideas about learning. The University offers general degrees, and it begins by offering a number of foundation courses. Its mathematics course 'will emphasize those concepts which underlie and are common to many areas of mathematics'. Its science course aims to 'show how science, technology and society are interrelated'. The aim of the technology course—'The Man-Made World'—is 'not only to explain and demonstrate the many aspects of the way engineers, designers and others do their job, but also to assess its impact upon us all'. The tendency of education at university level has been to move away from the single-subject degree to the multiple-subject degree. Now it moves on to the broader degree which crosses traditional subject boundaries. The shift in emphasis is not likely to be welcomed by everyone. Marghanita Laski, in discussing the early television programmes put out to supplement the foundation course in the Humanities, objected to the aim of the course—to present 'a total picture of man' by teaching about man's creative actions in art, music, history, philosophy and religious studies. 'This is not, or should not be, the language or the attitude of modern university-level studies.'[9] Nonetheless, these are the only terms on which a full use of open-network television is justified in an integrated teaching system. It cannot be concluded that this is the main reason for adopting this type of approach to education, but it is inevitable that the presence of broadcasters and educational technologists on course teams responsible for course content will exert an influence away from the highly specific and towards the general.

Equally inevitably, changes in educational administration and course content will bring changes in examination procedures, teacher training, and all aspects of teaching methods. The concept of the 'active classroom' and an increased interest in discovery methods are indications that the whole emphasis of educational method is changing. The swing is away from the teaching of information and towards the teaching of procedures: where and how to find the information, how to apply skills, how to solve problems. By aiming at the underlying procedures in any course of study, the new methodology eliminates the distinction between student and non-student, between child and mature adult, when faced with problems of living in society and coping with an increasing flood of information. We all need to understand how to work out problems, how to sort out relevant from irrelevant information, how to make our own priorities. We all need to know why we fail to solve some problems, rather than be provided with an infinite number of solutions. There is evidence that the new technology has an important part to play in this approach

to the learning process. Even the traditional concept of programmed instruction has given way to a discovery method
approach: 'It is misleading to say that programs typically or
ideally aim at a well-specified terminal behavior. It is rather the
case that they aim at a terminal repertoire of acceptable problem-
solving methods.'[10]

This tendency does not, of course, eliminate the need for a
structured system. It is an inefficient system of education which
simply exposes a child to life, and tells him to 'learn'. An English
speaker, set down in a totally Turkish- or Swahili-speaking environment, will certainly pick up Turkish or Swahili to a greater
or lesser degree through simple exposure. Disseminate the entire
11-year-old school population of England throughout France, and
they will probably learn as much French in six months as they
will learn in four years in England. The system would be effective
but inefficient, if we consider the many other claims upon the
students' time. Therefore, some sort of structured system is required; but the structure will hopefully be based upon an integrated system, in which methods, course content, examinations,
administration, and available technology are all interrelated.

Rethinking the Role of Technology

Developments such as these in the education sphere are most
convenient for the producers of hardware and software for the
new technology. Now the 'general interest' programme has some
relevance. The vast resources of the media can be set to work,
both with some chance of covering costs and making money,
and, this time, with educational justification. Terms such as
'enrichment' and 'direct teaching' have to be redefined in the
light of the broader approach to teaching. Should the technologists, however, claim that the educationists have simply come
over to their side of the fence, they are mistaken. The kind of
mass distribution materials which have been produced in the
past will not do for the role of technology in an integrated system.
In the past, the technology has been placed centrally in the teaching system—the tape or record course, the film series, the television
programme, the teaching machine programme, the filmstrip. The

rest of the system has been communicated in accompanying notes for the student or the teacher. Often, as with centrally produced language-teaching programmes on television and film, the accompanying material has contained the bulk of the teaching system. The technology has frequently been called upon to play a greater part in the teaching system than it can naturally handle, in order to demonstrate and sell its capabilities. The results have generally been unsatisfactory because, more often than not, the balance of the teaching system has been completely wrong. In a correctly balanced teaching system, the role of technology is undoubtedly more limited—but the limitation is all to the good. Each technological resource will be used only when it has a unique contribution to make to the learning process. It will not be required to perform beyond its capabilities. Most important, the technology will no longer be isolated, having to justify its use on its own merits; it will interlock with educational criteria and demands at each stage, and justify itself by the part it can play in a total teaching system.

Notes

1. John Scupham: 'Broadcasting and the Open University' *Journal of Educational Technology* No. 1 Vol. 1, Jan. 1970

2. Wilbur Schramm, Philip H. Coombs, Friedrich Kahnert, Jack Lyle: *The New Media: Memo to Educational Planners* UNESCO: IIEP, 1967, p. 98

3. Richard Hooper: 'A Diagnosis of Failure' *AV Communications Review* Vol. 17 No. 3, Fall 1969

4. John Scupham: *Broadcasting and the Community* Watts 1967, p. 164

5. G. O. M. Leith: 'Developments in Programmed Learning' p. 49 in *New Media and Methods in Industrial Training* (eds. J. Robinson & N. Barnes), BBC 1967

6. C. A. Wedemeyer: 'The Future of Educational Technology in the U.S.A.' in *Teaching and Television* (ed. Guthrie Moir), Pergamon 1967, p. 134

7. Jacques Ellul: *The Technological Society* Cape 1965, p. 6

8. E. W. H. Briault: *Learning and Teaching Tomorrow* National Council for Educational Technology Occasional Paper 2, 1969

9. Marghanita Laski: 'Hey Jude, or the Open University' in *The Listener* Vol. 85 No. 2197, May 1971

10. G. Pask and B. Lewis: 'Theory and Practice of Adaptive Teaching Machines' in *Teaching Machines and Programmed Learning* II (ed. R. Glaser) DAVI 1965

2 Technology and the Developing World

So far, we have looked at changes which are taking place in the education system; changes which emphasize the learning process rather than the teaching process, and the learner as a member of society rather than a receptacle for information. And we have seen that as the re-ordering of the education structure takes place, so technology can play a larger part within it.

Different Education Systems

Such discussion as has taken place on these subjects of change has usually been concerned with countries which are at a fairly advanced level of educational development. But what of the great proportion of the world which is concerned with educational development at a lower level? This is particularly relevant when we come to discuss the teaching of English, since it is those countries with less developed systems of education which require English most urgently as part of their development programmes. In these areas, it is of little use to describe education as 'the study of man and his place in society', or 'the individual and his potential', however admirable these objectives may be in absolute terms. Education in developing countries is related more directly to manpower requirements for economic development. Educational policies are secondary to manpower strategies which plan education and job provisions simultaneously.[1] In practice, there are many problems in achieving this kind of planning. Secondary school and university graduates are required urgently for agriculture, commerce, industrial expansion, government administration and the teaching profession. Having poured money into education to meet this demand, it is often the case that the economic expansion lags behind the educational expansion, and the educated find that they are unemployed. Supply and demand have to be kept in balance, and it is the current policy of aid donors to try to ensure the balance is maintained. The important point, however, is that in developing countries, such direct social connections can be made between supply and demand, and legislated for.

Before discussing the implications of this for an education system, it is useful to employ C. E. Beeby's classification of educational development.[2] He identifies four levels. The first level is characterized by simple rote-learning methods to teach basic skills, often imparted by poorly trained and ill-educated teachers. The second level of development introduces some kind of formal system of education. Rote-learning still predominates, but the teachers are slightly better educated and have some training. There is a curriculum which is fixed and centrally determined, and instruction is controlled rigidly by an inspectorate. The third level of development is based upon a teaching body which, because it is educated and trained, has more confidence in its superiority over the student body. The syllabus remains an officially recommended document, but teachers are prepared to venture outside it. Supplementary readers and simple classroom aids make an appearance. The basic skills are taught well, but there is little attempt to encourage creativity among students. The fourth level is reached where teachers are well-educated and well-trained; where educational institutions are free to plan their own systems of work and the teacher is autonomous inside his own classroom; where teaching methods encourage discovery procedures and problem-solving habits on the part of the learners.

It will be seen that the changes which are taking place in the emphasis of education, discussed in the first section, have relevance at the fourth level of development. Here, educating people for economic slots in society, with specialization at an early stage, has become less necessary. One can afford to take a broader approach to education at this level. It is here that the tension between education in the classroom and educational technology is most severe, since products for mass distribution have to relate to the method, grading and pacing—and often teaching-content —of each individual teacher in his classroom. And, as we have seen, the tension is being eased to some extent by adjustments within the education system. Changes in the approach to course content, to methods, and to the categorizing of students, allow for reappraisal of the total system, which, in turn, allows for technology to be accommodated more satisfactorily within it.

When we turn to lower levels of educational development, it is clear that the systems are different. Therefore we would expect the role of technology to be different.[3] The main difference lies in the degree of centralized control over the system. A central budgeting programme relates education to the economy much more directly than in developed countries, Frequently, both are related to politics much more closely. Issues such as regional development, university entrance requirements, the study of national history, the choice of a second language, or the provision for literacy among speakers of tribal dialects—decisions on such matters often have a political, rather than an educational basis. It is inevitable, therefore, that governments will wish to keep a fairly tight control upon a national educational system, even down to the minutiae of classroom procedures. Even if teachers were trained to the extent that they were able to teach creatively and experiment with methods and materials, there are often other reasons why this would be undesirable—it would strain other parts of the system. Similarly, too close attention to in-dividual tuition, the fragmentation of courses according to categories of student, would not only overburden other parts of the system—administration, materials provision and so on—but it is simply not a priority for countries faced with the problem of rapid mass education, with, possibly, massive drop-out at all levels. Politically and economically it makes sense to encourage (and sometimes enforce) uniformity in the education system at lower levels of development.

Naturally, this presents problems for educational innovation. It is not possible for development to occur in one sector of the system, which then jogs other sectors into reappraisal. Advance has to proceed on a broad front, and is all the more difficult to bring about as a result. It is rare to find the 'progressive' school, or the objective examination or the self-contained classroom at one level of the system, since these things are divisive. The 'different' school will raise questions of discrimination; the

objective test raises problems of teaching methods, textbooks,
teacher-training; the self-contained classroom, where it is introduced into primary schools, can cause chaos at the beginning
of conventional secondary education, with the constant need for
remedial schooling. Usually such innovations are not worth the
money and effort involved. Those concerned with the provision
of aid to developing educational systems are familiar with the
'pilot project' syndrome; far from piloting the entire educational
ship into more progressive waters, this phrase normally implies
containment within a landlocked harbour. The 'best thinking of
the educational profession' is therefore not required very often
for developing educational systems, since it can create more
problems for a uniform system than it solves.

A Different Role for Technology

Educational technology in developing countries, therefore, is not
likely to be welcomed as the great catalyst for change. Its implications for other parts of the system—which have produced tension
at the fourth and final level of development—can clearly be
regarded as a divisive influence. There are many examples in
the developing world of audio-visual aid systems and educational
television systems which have either been gifted by aid donors,
or purchased for their intrinsic glamour, and which have been
retained as prestige projects only, having hardly any effect upon
the system as a whole.

Nor are educational technologists likely to jump at the chance
of taking part in the education of the developing world. At the
fourth level of development, it is possible for them to influence
innovation in other parts of the system, in isolated classrooms,
certain universities, regional areas, and finally the whole system
of education. One can see this happening in England, for example.
But no such piecemeal progression is possible in education at
lower levels of development. Here, the technology has to conform;
it has to deal with what is, not with what might be. It cannot
say, 'Let us fill the villages with television sets and put out programmes in elementary hygiene and basic agriculture; you can
then bypass your expensive literary project, for who then will

need to read and write?' Such a project has its advocates, and they have yet to be proved wrong. But the political, social and economic ramifications of such radical proposals are probably so enormous that the governments would be quite correct to disregard them. Basic skills have to be acquired as they have in the developed world; there may be some speeding up of processes, but there will be no short cuts. The curriculum and syllabus are fixed textbooks are written or selected centrally; even pacing and grading are normally regulated. Central administration tends to be overloaded, teaching remains a low-status profession, and educational development often produces social tensions in the student body. These factors inevitably make classroom methods conservative. On the face of it, this is hardly the situation in which the unique powers of television or film can be used to best advantage; hardly the place for imaginative application of technology.

And yet, paradoxically, it is in the situation of low-level educational development that the conditions exist which educational technologists find ideal. In England it takes considerable persuasion and influence to get the autonomous teacher and the independent broadcaster round the same table; and it takes considerably more time and patience to blend the broadcaster's need for mass distribution with the teacher's highly specific requirements. In developing countries, the centrally controlled, authoritarian education system obviates the need for such prolonged courtship. Precisely because the system is centrally controlled it has a certain unity, and the introduction of technology can immediately influence the entire system, rather than remaining a fringe activity. Precisely because the system is national, uniform and authoritarian, the technology has the mass distribution it requires. Educationally, it cannot produce tension, since it has to operate within the terms of the system.

The most important point is to realize that the system, within which the technology is to function, is different from that of the fourth level of development. Hence, the role of the technology has to be different. It can carry out functions unthinkable in developed educational systems. Assumptions made about the use of technology in education in developed countries simply do not apply in areas of low-level development. For example, Chu and

Schramm's collection of studies of teacher attitudes to instructional television refer to American teachers in American schools.[4] It is not known whether such attitudes exist among less well-educated and less well-trained teachers elsewhere: fears that machinery will take away their occupations, fears that it will destroy their contact with students, suspicions as to its effectiveness. But in a centralized, authoritarian system, such attitudes play no part in decision-making; they do not form an obstacle to be overcome. It remains a valid principle that the technology should try to do what the teacher cannot do in his classroom. But at low-level educational development, the teacher cannot do a great many things. The role of the technology, therefore, is potentially much greater. John Scupham's comment, 'A broadcast can stimulate, but cannot itself undertake the dialectics of the classroom', becomes less valid. It is certainly not true of English language television programmes, as will be discussed later. Far more direct teaching is not only possible, but necessary. Where there is no laboratory equipment in schools, the media can do the experiments for the teacher. Where a textbook, and the methods it advocates, requires elucidation, the media can use the same textbook and the same methods; while teaching the students they simultaneously provide in-service training for the teachers. Teacher-training becomes one of the major functions of the new technology, because it operates within a uniform system at the same level of sophistication as the teacher in the classroom. This may not be using technology to its maximum potential, in the sense that a medium is not being exploited to its limits. But this is never the aim of technology; rather, it is there to serve efficient communication, which will always vary according to the intelligence, understanding, and social situation of the audience. The fact remains that the technology is being used to its maximum advantage as one component in a total educational system.

The problem of technology in developing educational situations has so far been a lack of clarity in specifying its objectives.[5] It has been difficult, therefore, to fit into a coordinated policy. The media are often brought into a country for prestige reasons, for entertainment; the country is then faced with the problem of lack of talent and a lack of money for recurrent expenditure or for buying filmed material or tapes from abroad. Under-utilized studios prompt a demand for cheap educational programming: we have TV, let's teach science or geography for secondary schools, mathematics for elementary schools. Definitions of requirements are easily made. Theoretical justifications, often based upon experiments carried out in developed educational systems, are nonetheless applied to developing countries, without any evidence that the same criteria apply. Since there is no clear-cut policy for the integrated use of the media, they assume the status of imported educational aids, and extremely expensive ones at that. Frequently the only software examples to hand are those produced for developed educational systems, which carry the stigma of 'enrichment', and can be seen to bear little relation to the fixed-syllabus system which prevails in the developing country. It is not surprising, therefore, that cost considerations predominate, and administrative problems—the authority controlling the media versus the authority controlling education—assume greater proportions than they need. Technology has to be sold to developing countries, not as an educational aid like textbooks and wallcharts, but as one element in a total educational system. Its exact contribution has to be specified precisely. To quote the UNESCO: IIEP Report: 'The time has come for planners to abandon the restrictive kind of thinking that asks such questions as: What can television do? What can radio do? What can films do? What can programmed learning do? These should be replaced by: What is the problem we want to solve and the conditions surrounding it? What combined system of teaching tools and learning experiences, then, will most efficiently meet it?'[6]

In short, the problem of technology at Beeby's first, second and third levels of educational development is exactly the same as its problem at the fourth level, discussed in the first section. Planning must take the form of establishing an organized system to deal with the problems of education, at whatever level. Each component of the system interrelates with all other components to produce a unified policy. Educational technology will have its place as part of a total strategy. The type of system, and therefore the role of technology, will depend upon non-educational factors —political, economic, social. But the approach to an integrated teaching system will be the same. In practice, this integration is easier to achieve at lower levels of development, where education tends to be centralized; it should be the objective at all levels, wherever an educational strategy is being planned.

What can the Technology do?

The quotation from the UNESCO: IIEP Report just used has to be looked at again. The first half suggests that we abandon 'the restrictive kind of thinking' which requires us to examine the potential of each medium of communication. The second half encourages us, rather, to examine the total problem and devise a total strategy. These two halves, however, are interconnected. As has been pointed out in a more recent UNESCO publication on the new methods and resources in education, we are still extremely ignorant about the potential of educational technology. If, in deciding upon an integrated strategy, we have to select one medium of communication rather than another, what criteria are available to help us? To ask: What can television do? What can radio do? are not idle questions, if the contribution of these media to a total strategy is to be efficient.

In a section on research needs, the UNESCO study suggests that we need answers to these questions:

'1. What is the optimum degree of student participation in a given learning situation?
2. What is the optimum structure and sequence?
3. What are the most appropriate media of communication?
4. What are the likely side-effects or unintended outcomes?
5. How much is lost by aiming at something less than the optimum which is both cheaper and more convenient?'[7]

Attempts have been made at answering these basic questions. Whether they are answered by controlled experiment, or whether they are dealt with empirically, on the basis of experience, they have to be considered in deciding upon a teaching strategy. Can a chemical reaction be understood by simple observation, or should a student be involved himself? What is the best order of presentation? Should we use film, possibly with a stop-frame device, or a televised live studio experiment? What ambiguities are likely to arise and how can they be avoided? If we cannot afford film, can we demonstrate the reaction by means of an animated diagram? What is lost in the communication if we do this?

When it comes to language teaching, these questions are equally fundamental. In some countries, the basic skills of literacy have been taught by television and by radio. These do not seem to be ideal means of teaching reading and writing skills; in an integrated strategy for literacy, would these media be given priority, or even be used at all? Film has frequently been used to teach speech—not only a command of language structure, but also features of pronunciation, intonation and stress. Again, would this medium be used for these tasks in an integrated teaching system? Tape-slide courses in language teaching abound on the market, offering to teach spoken language skills with visual, 'situational' stimuli. Many tape courses are prepared specifically for language laboratories. The technology is here placed centrally in the course, and the variety of other language skills are bundled into accompanying notes and textbooks. Would not this be rearranged in an integrated system of language teaching? The fault has been that the technique has often dictated the method, rather than the reverse. Tapes and language laboratories are suitable for pattern practice, structure drilling, pronunciation work: a tape course will therefore emphasize this aspect of language at the expense of other basic skills. Films and television can show language in situations; situational criteria dominate such courses, and there is little scope for drilling and mastering the structures which are merely observed. Nor are the skills of literacy in a language adequately dealt with; many film series assume that a reading ability is picked up simultaneously with an oral ability, without requiring special attention. Thus, new techniques have brought new misconceptions. The traditional textbook has always had the fault as a medium of emphasizing reading and writing skills at the expense of oral skills.

Now let us look at the five fundamental questions again, with relation to the problems of language teaching. First, we have to know the degree of student participation that is required in the various aspects of language learning. This raises questions of the active and passive knowledge of a language; of the role of initial presentation against regular practice of a language skill; of motor-perceptive skills as opposed to those skills which require thought and deliberation. It also raises the question of the type of participation by the learner—whether he participates as a result of habits, slowly acquired, or whether he participates by means of applying rules of language organization.

Second, we need to come to some conclusion about the structure and sequence of the learning process with regard to the various language skills. It is generally assumed that speech is primary and that other skills are best taught later. If we hold this view, should film or television, with their disadvantages in the practising of speech habits, be used in the early years of English? How do we sequence the teaching and drilling of listening skills with the teaching and drilling of speaking skills? How do we sequence both in relation to the teaching and drilling of the reading skill? Do we phase in each skill separately and try to link them later, or do we interlink them from the beginning? Is in fact a skill-structured course a realistic approach to language teaching?

Thirdly, decisions need to be made on how we teach what. Should the media introduce material which the teacher then practises? Or should the teacher introduce and let machinery handle mechanical speech practice? Are pre-reading skills and the more advanced skills of reading comprehension best left to the 'dialectic of the classroom' or can they be handled more efficiently by the media, or programmed teaching machines? What is the role of the visual element in language teaching? Are still pictures anything more than useful, artificial stimuli in the language teaching classroom, or do they have real value in relating language to situation? Teaching language in a classroom is inevitably artificial; we hold up a book to practise 'What's this?', knowing full well that everyone knows the answer. How far should technology be employed to make language more 'real', and how far can we expect students to accept the conventions of the classroom? Such questions will affect our choice of media.

Language is an inefficient communications system; ambiguity operates at every level. Even concrete objects, such as 'chair', have different connotations for different people. Given the situation of a teacher holding up a book, the structure, 'This is a book' can have a wide variety of connotations for a non-English-speaking class, from 'I'm showing you a yellow book' to 'Does this book belong to anyone?' A teacher in a classroom has a good chance of restricting ambiguities of this nature, due to the immediate feedback techniques at his disposal. The use of technology, however, runs the risk of involved ambiguities, without any immediate means of checking them. This is particularly true of visual media, employed in societies with their own perceptual sets. Design conventions, perspective, the basic problems created by a photographic or drawn representation of actual objects—these factors are most important in language learning. Each medium has its own conventions, and these can confuse an already ambiguous linguistic situation if the conventions are unknown. Students may have to be taught the editing conventions of film, the juxtaposition of long shots and close-ups on television, or the recognition of sound effects on tape or radio, before these media can be used in the teaching of language.

Lastly, we have to assess how much of a communication is lost by using imperfect means, which may be forced upon us for economic reasons. Can a still picture adequately convey 'walking', 'running', 'picking up'? Is this simply an extension of the last question—a matter of learning conventions? Is the teacher and blackboard qualitatively worse than a teacher with real objects he has brought to the classroom to refer to? Is one hour of group or choral drilling with a teacher qualitatively worse than drilling with a language laboratory? Where there are economic and administrative pressures on the system, actual knowledge about such compromises is extremely valuable.

On some of these issues, experimental work has been done.[8] On many of them, more work needs to be done, and to be done for each type of educational system at each level of development. This does not necessarily imply controlled experimentation, which is very often difficult to mount in developing countries. Experience, trials and revisions, empirical judgements—all help to come to some conclusions on these problems before planning a teaching strategy which incorporates the use of educational technology.

The remainder of this book deals with some of these issues in one small subject area, that of English language teaching, and the application of one medium—television. We have to know what television can do and what it can't do for the language-learning process. It is then up to the planners to decide whether they wish to incorporate it into their total strategy for English-language teaching. Some of its possibilities will only be usable at certain levels of educational development—this will depend upon the other components in the system at a particular level. What we aim for here is an inventory of television's potential uses in the language learning process.

Television has already been used in many countries for the teaching of languages. But it has been used in such a way as to conform to the prevailing theory and methodology of language teaching. This theory and methodology is currently being reassessed. Television language-teaching programmes have also tended to place themselves centrally in the total teaching situation, which has consequently been incorrectly balanced. The role of television has therefore to be reassessed from the point of view of the part it might play in a balanced, integrated teaching system. But first, we need to know more about the language-learning process itself. Before we discuss the technique, we need to look at the theory and the methodology.

Notes

1. Eli Ginzberg and Herbert A. Smith: *Manpower Strategy for Developing Countries; Lessons from Ethiopia* Columbia University Press 1967
2. C. E. Beeby: *The Quality of Education in Developing Countries* Harvard University Press 1966. Quoted in Schramm, Coombs, Kahnert, Lyle (1967) op. cit.
3. John Anderson: 'The Changing Nature of British Educational Aid' *Bulletin of the Institute of Development Studies* University of Sussex Vol. 3 No. 3, June 1971
4. Godwin C. Chu and Wilbur Schramm: *Learning from Television: What the Research Says*. NAEB 1967, pp. 68–9
5. Henri Dieuzeide: 'Educational Technology and the Development of Education' in *British Journal of Educational Technology* No. 3 Vol. 2
6. Schramm, Coombs, Kahnert, Lyle: op. cit. p. 64
7. Norman MacKenzie, Michael Eraut, Hywel C. Jones: *Teaching and Learning: an introduction to new methods and resources in higher education* UNESCO: IIEP 1967, p. 153
8. For example: Helen Coppen: *A Survey of British Research in Audio-Visual Aids* National Committee for Audio-Visual Aids in Education, 1968

3 Language Teaching: Theories and Methods

Language Programmes on Television

Television has not taken to language teaching with that warmth and creativity with which it has embraced other subjects in the curriculum. In looking for explanations for this situation, the tendency is to point to the inherent deficiencies of television itself. This is the case even among the broadcasters. Kenneth Fawdry, in examining the reasons for the lack of language-teaching programmes on television, says that this is 'not because television is not a good medium for these, but because its advantages in school conditions, over radiovision or recorded radio programmes plus pamphlets are questionable; whereas in mathematics or science these advantages are outstanding'.[1] John Scupham thinks that 'the task of language-teaching programmes can only be that of initial presentation. Consolidation and assessment, and steady practice of what has been learnt, must lie with the teacher.'[2] In 1965, a survey was published on television language-teaching programmes in nineteen countries signatory to the European Cultural Convention. Almost all these countries have educational systems at Beeby's fourth level of development.[3] They offered few programmes for complete beginners; most instruction was geared to students with two or three years or prior study of the language; and there was then a large gap until the stage of 'preuniversity cultural teaching'. In explaining these gaps, Raymond Hickel, the editor of the survey, asks whether the medium itself may be at fault: 'Is this deliberate or fortuitous, or is it due to an inherent lacuna in the television presentation of language teaching?'[4]

These misgivings about the use of television in teaching language stem from the supposition that 'language teaching' is a well-defined, unchanging factor; any inability to accommodate television to its demands must therefore be the fault of television. But language teaching has not in fact remained unchanging; it has changed and developed over the years, as theories and methodologies have won widespread approval and then been eclipsed by other ideas. When we examine the kind of television programmes for teaching language over the past decade, it is necessary to bear in mind the climate of theory and methodology of language teaching during that period. If the technique has failed to serve the method, the fault may lie with the methods themselves. Not that the method should therefore be changed simply to suit the technique. Rather in reassessing the method, it may be possible to incorporate the technique—in this case, television—more happily in the total system, and thus use it to better advantage.

We should consider two features of programmes aimed at teaching language.

(i) In American programmes for teaching English overseas, 'inducing the viewer to react to stimuli' has been a strong element. Lengthy periods are spent with a television teacher conducting drills from the screen, cueing the audience for repetitions and substitutions rather in the manner of 'pattern practice', the type of exercise which dominated American audio-lingual methodology for twenty years. The cues may be verbal or visual; their aim is to make the learner produce automatically the structure being dealt with in the programme.

(ii) A second feature of programmes for teaching language has been their demonstration of 'language as behaviour'. Television, the argument runs, enables us to structure for the viewer the contexts within which language behaviour occurs. Language behaviour occurs haphazardly in life; for the purposes of teaching we need to be able to examine it, break it down and serve it up in a structured form. We can then grade it, sequence it, and select language items to fit each stage. Television can present 'natural' situations within which language occurs—with no forced intonation patterns; no contrived action e.g. opening and closing doors to illustrate 'he is opening', 'she is closing'; no need to hold up a book and ask 'What's this?' when the answer is obvious. 'The more "real" the language is to the learner, the greater its teaching value will be.'[5] Television is able to do what the classroom teacher can never do—and that is to present language together with a great deal of its extra-linguistic environment.

The Theoretical Background

Features of television language-teaching programmes such as those mentioned above lead us to a discussion of the extent to which the methodology of such television programmes reflects the orthodox methodology of classroom teaching at a particular time, and of the relations between language-teaching methodology on the one hand and prevailing theories in linguistics and psychology on the other. In particular, we shall consider recent theoretical ideas about language acquisition, about the description of languages, and about the notions of *competence* and *performance* in language. And in our discussion we shall need to distinguish between notions whose influence was largely confined to either America or Europe and those which have been more universally accepted.

The original impetus of linguistics during the first three decades of this century, in America as in Europe, was above all *descriptive*; it was concerned with observing language as it is spoken and written, with studying and describing the patterns of sound, of grammar and of meaning in every language of the world. Parallel with the growth of these basic tenets of linguistics there occurred a change in language teaching from being solely the handmaiden of literary and historical studies to being concerned in addition with practical ability in using the contemporary language. Improved linguistic descriptions helped to encourage improved teaching of practical language use. In particular, new linguistic descriptions of *spoken* language were of assistance in the rise of the 'direct method', the language methodology which forbade the teacher to make any use of the learner's mother-tongue. The sheer practical difficulty of sustaining direct method techniques in the classroom led to the development, during the period 1925–45, of various modifications to it; the acceptance that sometimes the learning may be helped by a few sentences in the learner's language; the division of the total language learning task into a large number of teaching items and the arrangement of these into graded sequences; the deliberate selection of particular teaching inventories of grammar and vocabulary items; and the development of 'situational' teaching techniques, with the aim of making the teaching and learning as meaningful and realistic as was possible in the essentially artificial circumstances of the classroom.

From the publication in 1933 of the book entitled *Language*, by the American linguist Leonard Bloomfield, a fresh strand of linguistic thought emerged which had great influence in the United States and which culminated, as far as language teaching is concerned, in a methodology (the *audio-lingual method*) consciously and deliberately based on theoretical ideas in linguistics and psychology.[6]

Bloomfield's linguistic principles included the notion that *speech* is primary, *writing* is secondary: the study of spoken language was to be rigorous and scientific; only observable facts were to be included, so that linguistics was to be largely concerned with the analysis of large quantities of spoken language, transcribed into written form. From this data the structural patterns of grammar and of sounds were to be discovered by the linguist. (This school of thought became known as American or Bloomfieldian structuralist linguistics.) But two further ideas were contained in Bloomfield's work which were to prove important for American language teaching. The first was the notion that *meaning* is so elusive, so difficult to observe, so inaccessible to structural analysis, so mentalistic, that it was probably not appropriate as the subject of a scientific methodology. The second was Bloomfield's description of conversation (i.e. the language used when people talk to each other) as having features similar to those of *stimulus* and *response* in the study of psychology—one speaker's utterance acts as a stimulus to the hearer, whose reply is a response to that stimulus.

In the next twenty years, these ideas became increasingly central to principles of language learning and teaching in the United States, until in the nineteen-fifties the package of ideas and techniques known as the *audio-lingual method* became the dominant, orthodox methodology. What were the fundamentals of the audio-lingual method? First, that sound language teaching must be based on Bloomfieldian structuralist linguistics as far as its language content was concerned, and on behaviourist psychology (and in particular, on stimulus-response conditioning theory) as far as its principles of learning and teaching were concerned. This was a statement of faith, not the result of inquiry or experiment: it seemed to those concerned self-evident that these two theories must constitute the best basis for teaching and learning languages. From these articles of faith there followed certain practical consequences. Teaching was to be essentially mechanistic in its approach, replicating with human learners the conditioning and habit-forming techniques which have been so successful in animal-training experiments. Learning was to be 'over-learning'—hence pattern-practice drills of inordinate length; meaning was subordinate to mimicry and memorization; the language learned was almost exclusively the spoken language of everyday converse; mechanical aids, including not only tape recorders and language labs, but also teaching machines and programmed instruction were to be used whenever possible.

The most extreme intervention of behaviourist psychology into the world of language learning was the publication by the Harvard experimental psychologist B. F. Skinner of his book *Verbal Behaviour* (1957). In this book Skinner carried across into a discussion of human language the main concepts and terminology of behaviourist psychology—stimulus, response, reinforcement, deprivation, etc. His aim was to control and predict verbal behaviour by observing and manipulating the physical environment of the learner. By monitoring the variety of stimuli which affect the speaker at any given moment, and by checking the resultant responses, he believed it was possible to analyse verbal behaviour into identifiable units. Skinner does not work with the notion of an independent entity, the 'mind', which controls language, and his reason is at least partly because what we can know of the mind is limited to our observation of its behavioural output. For him, 'thinking' is nothing more than 'talking with concealed musculature'.[7]

It is worth noting that Skinner's book had very little impact in Europe, where the brands of psychology familiar to language teachers were those of Piaget and Watson. Similarly, Bloomfieldian structural linguistics was not accepted in Europe even though in the United States it was the almost universal orthodoxy. But in the United States, Skinner's book was the last straw. It became the target of massive and destructive criticism by Noam Chomsky, whose linguistic theories, known as transformational-generative grammar, already challenged the linguistic establishment, who now added to this a sophisticated and damaging critique of orthodox behaviourist psychology, in the form of a review of Skinner's book.

Chomsky objected to the application of behavioural analysis to language acquisition and to the vagueness with which the behaviourist terminology related to language functions. Behaviourism itself was suspect, since, Chomsky said, 'It seems that there is neither empirical evidence nor any known argument to support any specific claim about the relative importance of "feedback" from the environment and the "independent contribution of the organism" in the process of language acquisition.'[8] In other words, do children learn their language by exposure to the same environmental stimuli as their elders, and by responding as their elders do? Or does the child have some inbred 'language faculty' which enables him to process the language data he hears in such a way as to reproduce and build upon it? Paradoxically, it is simple observation of a child's language behaviour which tends to confirm Chomsky's view that a child has a natural ability to decode and encode language information on the basis of unconscious generalizations he makes about it. A child will produce 'thrub' rather than 'srub', since the former conforms to the sound system of English; he will apply recognized pluralization rules to nonsense words which he has never encountered before. It is this creative ability in language which the behaviourist theory of language acquisition does not account for.

This internal knowledge of language Chomsky terms *competence*, and he contrasts it with the actual use an individual makes of this ability, his *performance*. Chomsky relates the speaker's performance to his underlying competence which enables him to judge the grammaticality of the linguistic data he is hearing or producing. There is an important theoretical difference in the role accorded to the mind of the producer and the receiver in Chomsky's theory, compared with Bloomfieldian structural linguistics, which based its descriptions on the analysis of performance, ignoring the role of the individual's creativity and competence.

These, then, have been some of the linguistic theories under discussion since television was first employed to teach English as a foreign language in the nineteen-fifties. Television programmes were based upon different methods of teaching English, which reflected, on occasion, elements of one, or several, theories. Further, the economic and technological strength of the United States ensured that many of the innovations in the use of television began there and thus brought to Europe and elsewhere examples of language-teaching methodology which were not current outside the U.S.A. But the teacher in the classroom or the textbook writer tends to be pragmatic: he will use a method which seems to work—and the method may owe something to more than one theoretical viewpoint. American structuralist theory gave rise, as we have seen, to language-teaching methods which proceeded in the belief that language acquisition was basically a question of habit-formation, and that techniques of stimulus and response were all that were required from the teacher, or from the language-laboratory tape as a substitute for the teacher. Yet in a metaphorical sense the use of stimuli to evoke responses remains an important element in all modern language-teaching classes and courses—even in those which reject most of the structuralist-behaviourist approach.

Chomsky's work on transformational-generative grammar may have little obvious relevance to the teacher of English (that is certainly Chomsky's own view)[8] but his attack on the behaviourist approach to language acquisition and description does have implications for any methods that are based upon such an approach. For example, pattern-practice drills, of the type used in audio-lingual courses and included for reasons of psychological theory, involve long and tedious application before the 'habit' can be said to be 'formed'. If Chomsky's view is correct, and if the conscious mental processes of the learner can be called upon to speed up his acquisition of new language material, then it would be reasonable to seek a method which would incorporate this fact. Such an approach is assumed in the use of terms like 'cognitive-code learning', or 'conscious rule-generalization', though these terms have not yet been erected into a 'method' as such. Indeed, some language teachers feel that even if the learner is encouraged consciously to apply rules in order to produce an utterance, the speech act as a whole has to be made automatic. In which case, all that has changed is the terminology: 'the formation of a new habit system' has simply been replaced by 'the reorganization of automatic cognitive processes'.

We have already mentioned the use of 'situational' teaching as a normal, standard procedure, intended to help the teacher to be as meaningful and realistic as possible in his classroom teaching. It is worth noting that this commitment to meaning is parallel to the insistence, in European linguistics (e.g. the Prague School, or in the work of J. R. Firth and his successors) that meaning is central to the study of language. Thus, teachers who wished to invoke the authority of linguistics for their practices in the language teaching classroom could do so. Indeed, there is some evidence that Firth's notion of *context of situation* (i.e. those features of the total environment of a language event which at any given moment influence the choice of language) has been borrowed by some writers of courses, especially audio-visual courses, and of television programmes.

For instance, a wide range of 'contexts of situation', presented visually to the learner, can immediately place the utterance in its extra-linguistic environment. However, problems arise in those teaching courses which try to relate *all* language to the environment in which it is used, and which ask the learner to discover intuitively an understanding of the language from this association of language and context of situation. A great proportion of our verbal behaviour is 'intraverbal';[9] that is, it is stimulated by other language, unrelated to the nonpersonal elements in the context. On occasion, we do react verbally to situations outside ourselves: asking someone to close the door, asking for something in a shop, commenting on a football match. But this type of speech activity, and methods based upon it, can only account for a relatively small proportion of our potential language output. Nonetheless, before dismissing the idea of context of situation we should recall that even such a formal language function as reported speech is usually dealt with in class by reference to the time-gap between reported action and the report, and the relationship between the reporter and the person reported upon, i.e. to frequently occurring features of the context of situation.

Language Teaching Methods

What is to be made of all this, of the conflicting claims of rival theories and their changes of emphasis and direction, by the classroom teacher, the course writer, the radio producer, the television scriptwriter? Faced with the problem of producing a total system for teaching language, and allocating roles to the various elements within that system, what he would like would be a single corpus of linguistic information to disseminate, and a single theory and method to tell him how this aim might best be achieved. This is far from being the case in language teaching. Arguments abound over one of the fundamental questions: what to include in a course and what to leave out—i.e. selection of material; there are problems over the most effective way to sequence that which has been selected for inclusion—i.e. the grading of material. Then there is considerable disagreement over the best way to apply the method we adopt—i.e. the presentation of the material; and, as we have seen, there is considerable argument over the type of participation required of the learner in his understanding and manipulation of language material. It will be useful to see how the teachers and writers of modern language courses deal with these four problem areas of *selection, grading, presentation* and *participation*, relating our discussion where possible to methods we have touched on briefly in this section. Certain methodological 'principles' seem to have become established in the practice of language teaching—including language teaching by television. As theories and methods are reassessed, these principles, upon which much practical work is based, may need to be looked at again.

Selection and Grading of Language

Most audio-lingual, audio-visual and television language courses emphasize the primacy of the spoken language, often ignoring completely the reading and writing skills. It is often said in defence of this sequence of stages that this is a 'natural' progression, reflecting the sequence in which a child acquires his first language. The literate skills, it is said, are easier to approach from a firm grounding in the spoken language.

On the face of it, it seems unnecessary to erect this idea into a principle, irrespective of the situation in which the language is being taught. Some learners may wish to read Russian literature, or to write Chinese characters, who will never wish to speak or listen to those languages. Even though they may be a small minority, they demonstrate the inadvisability of being dogmatic. In a second language or a foreign language situation, the relative emphasis accorded to the various skills in our selection of material will presumably vary according to the degree to which students are likely to use them. There may be a good case for mixing the four basic language skills from the beginning. As Saporta points out, the capitalization of nouns in German, or the place of the apostrophe in /boys/boy's/boys'/, are graphological devices which make linguistic points more clearly in writing than in speech, yet they are of obvious use in teaching the accurate use of spoken forms.[10]

In those courses which advocate that reading and writing should be delayed, there are always enormous problems of phasing in these skills. An emphasis upon speech has led to a number of classroom teaching devices of doubtful utility. The choral drills and group drills and endless repetition of sentence patterns have sometimes led to exhausted teachers and apathetic students. It is here that some distinction needs to be made between *teaching* procedures which can involve the mental capacity of the students to a greater extent and *practice* procedures (in which certain types of stimulus-response work may be of use).

The teaching of pronunciation, too, often fails to find the balance between the overformalization of using phonetic script (teaching *about* language), and the mindless unmotivated repetition of minimal pairs. Where there are no difficulties between a learner's mother-tongue and the foreign language, explanation of articulatory movements, and phonetic symbols for reference, may help to identify and clarify the difficulty for the learner.

Together with the principle of the 'primacy of speech', the idea has developed among some authorities that the language to be taught should be sequenced and controlled as rigidly as possible. This may be done contextually, from beginnings in the classroom situation, later bringing in the outside world. Or it may be achieved on the basis of ease of demonstration and structure-contrast: for example, present continuous actions are more demonstrable than present simple actions, and should precede them and be contrasted with them: -s plural endings are taught separately from -z plural endings and -ize endings. The structure syllabus becomes the rock upon which the entire language course is founded. It helps to control inputs and monitor outputs as closely as possible, thus developing correct behaviour step by step.

The breaking down of the material to be learnt into small units is a technique contrary to the idea of creativity in language, discussed earlier. As Jerrold Katz writes: 'We do not credit a person with mastery of a foreign langage if he is only able to understand those sentences which he has previously been taught. The test of fluency is whether he can understand those sentences that he has not been taught.'[11] Just as a child's mind will apply 'rules' to available language data—*man* to *mans* or *played* to *leaved*—until new data becomes available, so any language learner is able to build upon data by classifying it and applying the classifications to further data.

The great problem with a solely structure-based course is that the rigid control has to phase out within a short time, since the teacher cannot hope to control all the language stimuli the student will receive. Clearly there has to be some grading and sequencing of the material for teaching purposes; but the material need not be a detailed list of the raw language data itself, so much as procedures to assist the learner's mind in dealing with this data. There are parallels here with the discovery methods currently being advocated in other subject areas such as mathematics and science. If it is argued that language is not an information-subject, but a skill-subject, it needs to be emphasized that we are here talking of teaching procedures as opposed to practice procedures. An understanding of the systems of language has to precede the automatization of these systems in the learner by constant practice. This distinction needs to be borne in mind when we discuss the teacher's method of presentation of the material, and how we expect the learner to learn and reproduce it.

Presentation and Learning of Language

Partly in reaction against the grammar-translation method of teaching, the principle has become established of teaching a linguistic item by association with its extralinguistic context. This, as any language teacher will agree, can be a highly ambiguous process. First, there may be ambiguity in the ways the teacher and the learner understand words denoting simple objects, such as 'lamp' or 'bread', especially where the teacher and learner come from different cultural backgrounds. Second, there may be ambiguity in structural concepts such as 'at', 'let's', 'ago', or such time-phrases as 'yesterday' or 'every morning'. These are examples taken from the early stages of English language teaching; the ambiguities are obviously compounded when we reach the stage of abstractions or 'idea-words', such as 'friend', 'autumn', 'happy'; or such structural concepts as 'must/have to/ need', or the intricacies of reported speech. Many teachers spend a great deal of time in class attempting to iron out these ambiguities by direct association procedures. In the long run, there can still be no guarantee that they have been completely eliminated until the correct reference item is used unambiguously in a given situation.

Direct association procedures, then, being inherently prone to ambiguity, often obscure what the mind seeks to understand clearly. As a teaching instrument, they are therefore inefficient. Translation procedures are often less ambiguous, though these are frowned upon, for various reasons, by teachers. Yet where translation produces clear understanding, it cannot be dismissed. Where mother-tongue explanation helps understanding, there seems no good reason why it should not be used. These are valid procedures for *teaching*. As *practice* procedures, however, they are probably not so effective.

Teaching and Practice Procedures

Whatever theory may be preferred by the teacher, he has no control over the method the student himself will employ in order to master a particular feature. Any adult who has studied a foreign language knows that his learning is helped by organizing the language data in his mind, and by classifying the material he is learning according to rules which can then be applied to further data. There seems no reason why children learning a foreign language should find these procedures any less helpful. But again, we must distinguish learning from practice procedures. We cannot operate verbally by consciously applying rules, any more than we can operate by translating every utterance mentally. What we need is practice. Some of this practice can be obtained by forms of drilling—in particular this is true for the closed systems of language, such as inflection of person and number and the formal features of the tenses. More complex practice will involve the use of learned rules in a variety of real communication situations, rather than in structure drills. For reading and writing skills, it will be possible to provide almost all the required situations within the classroom itself. It is doubtful whether this can be done, however, for the more intricate contexts which surround the listening and speaking functions. Probably it can never be done outside the social situations in which the language is used as a mother-tongue or lingua franca. Certainly, gross simplification of these situations can be constructed in and around the classroom, and used for practice purposes. These artificial situations are what Pit Corder calls 'simulated contexts',[12] and he suggests that television can be of greatest use here. But it has to be remembered that these situations are useful for practice, rather than as part of the teaching process. We will discuss later whether television has any part to play in the practice of language skills as opposed to the teaching of an understanding of language.

To say that teaching procedures will allow a student more freedom to organize the language he learns and to apply it, does not imply a return to grammar-translation methods. The aim is that the student should clearly understand the systems which operate in the language before making them a matter of automatic response by practice. This understanding may be achieved in a number of ways, which may include translation, mother-tongue explanation, or the intelligent use of rules, which, themselves, might be presented in several ways. Inductive learning may be an effective way of doing this: the student, with the teacher's help, comes to his own understanding of the system in operation, by examining the data presented to him. The difference is that, while methods based upon structuralist-behaviourist ideas merely assume that this takes place, a more efficient method makes certain that it does. Nor can this approach deal effectively with *all* types of language systems—sometimes a more deductive approach will be simpler and more effective. As far as teaching is concerned, then, we should expect to see 'a constant interplay of learning by analogy and by analysis, of inductive and deductive processes— according to the nature of the operation the student is learning'.[13] As for internalizing the systems to the point of automatic response, practice procedures may include mimicry-memory techniques, pattern drilling, and the creation of contexts for language use, according to the nature of the operation the student is practising.

Let us now return to the role of television. It is clear that some programmes, particularly those centred upon the dogmatic pursuit of a particular linguistic or psychological theory, have 'taught' very little. 'To show language in action, language as behaviour' is a practice procedure, not a teaching technique, and it is in any case hard to imagine that a 20-minute programme, transmitted once or twice each week, provides anywhere near the intensity of practice required for successful language learning. Whatever audience such programmes were aimed at—whether a school class with a teacher or a home student with a textbook—it is hard to see what contribution the programmes have made to the total teaching situation.

In fact, in an eclectic approach to language teaching, where there is a 'constant interplay' of learning techniques, depending upon the type of operation being learned and practised, is there any role for television at all? This is the question to be examined in the next chapter.

Notes

1. Kenneth Fawdry: 'School Television in the BBC' in Guthrie Moir: op. cit. p. 24
2. John Scupham: op. cit. 1967, p. 189
3. Beeby: op. cit. 1966
4. Raymond Hickel: *Modern Language Teaching and Television* Council of Europe 1965, p. 30

5. S. Pit Corder: *English Language Teaching and Television* Longmans 1960, p. 51

6. Leonard Bloomfield: *Language* New York, Holt 1933

7. B. F. Skinner: *Verbal Behaviour* Appleton-Century-Crofts 1957

8. Noam Chomsky: Review of Skinner's 'Verbal Behaviour' in *Language* 35 No. 1, 1959

9. See Pit Corder: op. cit. (1960), pp. 78–81

10. Sol Saporta: 'Applied Linguistics and Generative Grammar' in *Trends in Language Teaching* (ed. A. Valdman) McGraw-Hill 1966, p. 85

11. Jerrold J. Katz: 'Mentalism in Linguistics' in *Language* 40 No. 2 1964

12. See Pit Corder: op. cit. (1960), pp. 44–55

13. Wilga M. Rivers: 'Patterns and Creativity in Language Learning' *Forum* Vol. VIII No. 6 1971

4 The Language Skills

One single method for language teaching will not do. An eclectic approach is required because the nature of the language material is eclectic. Anyone faced with the problem of writing a television series to teach language has to come to terms with this eclecticism. To write a course 'to teach English' on television is not possible; large assumptions have to be made and additional material put into an accompanying textbook. Even textbooks, however, rarely come to terms with the eclectic nature of language material. Some assume an ability to read English script from the very moment the spoken language is started. Some include exercises which require a written response at an early stage, without any preparation in the writing skill. The majority of modern courses tend to emphasize speech to the exclusion of other skills. Two reasons are normally given: first, that this reflects a way a child learns his first language; second, that it is easier to teach reading and writing upon a sound basis of a command of the spoken language. Consequently, teachers are often advised to teach the first year of language instruction orally, and to bring in reading and writing in the second year. This has led to exhausted teachers and students endeavouring to get through five hours a day of spoken language work. And it has led to later problems of phasing in reading and writing abilities to catch up with the aural/oral abilities.

Assembling a Language Course

Television and textbook courses which have been put together, or synthesized, in this way, are the result of an inadequate analysis of the language requirements which need to be met. Such an analysis is normally based upon a division of language material into skills. Four areas are usually identified: listening, speaking, reading, writing. The listening skill is required in the early stages for the correct recognition of sounds and sentences for the purpose of imitation; in later stages, listening comprehension exercises may be given. A speaking skill involves correct pronunciation and correct repetition of given structures in the early stages; in later stages it involves the production of the correct response to a given contextual stimulus. The reading skill involves the recognition of written words. The writing skill involves the correct representation of these words on paper. Such an analysis provides clearly defined areas where different types of skills are required from the language learner. Such an analysis allows the course writer—textbook or television—to decide where he will concentrate his efforts, and where he will make assumptions about the learner's other sources of instruction. The English language teaching market abounds in examples of coursebooks which have been produced on the basis of this kind of analysis. Books for written comprehension work, books to teach spoken English, handwriting books: such books deal with a particular section of the analysis of language material. Where a synthesis has been attempted—in general coursebooks, or in ELT television series—each of the four skills has had to be balanced in some way in its relation with the others. And it is here —in achieving a synthesis—that most trouble is caused. There are no general principles available for setting a balance for the four skills. To say that speech is primary is only to say that it seems easier to read a word and write it, if you can already say it. Perhaps experimentation would determine the truth of this hypothesis. Such an explanation, however, serves only to justify the course which emphasizes speech to the neglect of the other skills. A textbook which teaches through the written word would have to make assumptions about the learners' need to listen to and to speak the material. It must decide whether to make provision for these skills, perhaps in accompanying tapes, or to neglect them entirely. A television series which aims 'to show language in action, language as behaviour' only touches upon the listening skill, and a decision has to be made on the provision of material for the other three skills in ancillary material.

Compromise is therefore the most prominent feature of a synthesized language teaching course, whatever medium is employed. This is not alleviated by a four-skill analysis of the language data to be taught, by artificially separating them, and then attempting to introduce them in a teaching strategy according to an arbitrary view of their relative importance. There is no reason why writing should be any less important, or more difficult to learn and to teach, than reading; or reading than speaking. The majority of educational processes begin with the most simple and move to the more complex. An arbitrary division of language data into four areas of skills does not achieve this form of progression. It makes sense to begin language teaching with the simplest operations and to grade the material towards the more difficult. This often means cutting across the division of skills in the data. Copying words, for example, is a simple task over which students often make mistakes. It requires an ability to read and write. Repeating words after a teacher is, again, a simple operation, involving listening and speaking abilities. These functions involve little mental effort but are essential parts of language acquisition. Certain other language functions are perhaps more difficult: dictation, for example, involves listening and writing; reading aloud involves reading and speaking. These skills are themselves less difficult than creating spoken utterances, following a lecture, taking notes, or skipping through a science book for information. There is, therefore, a progression inherent in the language data to be acquired, according to the degree of difficulty, or mental involvement, in each language function. A second progression might be seen in the amount of practice each function requires for mastery, after an initial understanding of it has been achieved.

A synthesized language course should reflect this type of progression, rather than attempt to teach each type of skill in turn, or, as often happens, to emphasize one skill and let the others look after themselves. The result is eclectic, and more accurately reflects the eclectic nature of language itself. The best synthesized course will be that which can most happily tie the various skills together at each level of difficulty by a judicious choice of content. In the classroom, an eclectic course will relieve teacher and students from whole periods of spoken drills or reading work, and will help motivation and understanding by placing each separate language activity in its total context of language acquisition. For the writer of television language programmes, an eclectic approach will allow the use of the medium for a number of different language activities within each programme, rather than using television in one small area and relying upon an ancillary textbook for everything else. Such an approach is also ideally suited to current developments in television techniques, as will be discussed in a later section.

A Course Analysis

Before synthesis comes analysis. We have to look at each skill from the point of view of a progression of difficulty, or the amount of mental involvement required from the learner. This does not imply that the motor-skills, such as copying, or repeating heard language, should necessarily be learnt without mental involvement. The learner, as has been discussed in a previous section, requires an understanding of the language functions he is acquiring. Imitation, pre-reading games, or the formation of letter-shapes are learnt more readily if the student understands the reason behind them. A clear differentiation between teaching and practice procedures needs to be made here.

Another factor to be borne in mind is the difference between the productive skills of speaking and writing, and the receptive skills of listening and reading. The difference lies mainly in the need for the teacher to monitor the learning process. Control of the productive skills is self-evident in the actual production of spoken or written language data. The receptive skills, however, can normally only be checked by the learner employing productive skills. We cannot know if something is understood unless the learner tells us so; and if his productive ability is inadequate, it is difficult accurately to monitor his command of the receptive skills. Other means have to be found which do not involve the use of speaking or writing. This problem, as we shall see, becomes important when we consider the use of television in language teaching, and wish to incorporate systems for allowing the viewer-learner to check his progress.

Language Realization: Sounds and Symbols

The level of language requiring least mental involvement is that of language realization in speech and writing. This is the behaviourist's raw data of language—what he can observe. The phonological realization of language applies most obviously to the skills of listening and speaking. A listening ability requires the recognition of different sounds in the language. The difficulties for learners of English will vary according to the sound system of their mother-tongue and to what extent it corresponds with that of English. In addition to recognizing the various phonological contrasts in the English sound system, the learner will also need to recognize different varieties of English speech, such as American-English differences, and different styles—the lecture, formal and informal conversation, and so on. The speaking skill involves an ability to produce the features of the English sound system, to make the necessary phonemic contrasts, and to produce the features of intonation and stress peculiar to English. The skills of reading and writing also involve, though to a lesser extent, an ability to recognize and produce the sound system of English. The field of phonics is of relevance here, the relationship between sounds and spellings, in such exercises as reading aloud, or taking dictation.

The graphological realization of language plays a major part in the skills of reading and writing. The learner has to be able to recognize the various written symbols of English and the meaning of punctuation marks. He may require practice in viewing script from left to right. He will also require practice in understanding various forms of written material—print, handwriting styles, various type-faces. He will need to practise various forms of reading techniques, from slow, intensive study to rapid, skipping speed. To achieve mastery of the writing skill, the learner has to practise the formation of English letters and the correct use of punctuation marks. Depending upon his own native writing-system, he may need practice in left-to-right hand movements, and he may possibly have to develop a different way of holding a writing instrument. Decisions will have to be made about the learning of a handwriting style—whether a particular form should be selected, or whether the learner should be left to develop his own style upon a learnt basis of printed letter forms.

The production and reception of language information, phonological and graphological, does not involve deep understanding of the systems which operate in the language. At this level of language skill, the learner is required to hear, to imitate correctly, and, in the case of written material, to read and copy correctly. It is then a matter of constant practice until these skills are adequately mastered.

Language Organization: Grammar

Greater mental involvement is required at the next level of difficulty in acquiring language skills—the learning of the grammatical systems which operate in English. Again, for the purpose of analysis, it is useful to look at each skill in turn. In practice, the listening and speaking skills are often combined at this level, though there are differences in the kind of language data to be acquired. A learner with a knowledge of the grammatical system of English as it operates in listening can recognize the form of the utterances he hears. There are a number of particular problems, however, attendant upon teaching this ability to recognize. For example, we normally get only one chance to recognize any one piece of language data which we hear—we cannot check back on it as we can with written material. The learner must become accustomed to this kind of instant recognition. A further problem in teaching the listening skill is the question of checking comprehension. In many instances, evidence of actual comprehension may be obscured by the learner's inability to *produce* this evidence —in speech. True-false answer formats, which, though they require an ability to recognize elements of the written system, do not require any production on the part of the learner, may be of use here.

To use correctly the grammatical systems of English in speech, the learner needs to be presented with the data in a graded form. He will need to be led to make generalizations about the systems in operation in each section of the data he hears and imitates, and to apply these generalizations to further data in speech. Situations will be devised for the learner to practise his command of the grammatical systems, until the point is reached where he can respond automatically to the stimuli—verbal or environmental—which are presented to him.

The acquisition of the grammatical systems for the skills of reading and writing presents few special problems, since the structure syllabus will, to a large extent, follow that of the speaking/listening skills. However, certain sections will need to emphasize the differences which exist between structures normally found in spoken language, and those more appropriate to the written form. Again, the learner will need to be taught to generalize from the written data he reads, and to apply such generalizations to new data.

So far, we have discussed two levels of language material from the point of view of a progression of difficulty. The first was that of the raw language information which we receive and produce in speech and writing. The second, more complex level, was that of the grammatical systems, which enable a learner to decode and encode the raw information into meaningful units. We now come to the third level of difficulty—that of meaning.

Meaning—Teaching and Practice

Speech and writing originate in the mind of the speaker/writer who wishes to communicate something. The listener/reader wishes to understand such communications. The phonology and graphology of English, and the grammar of English, are common to both the speaker/writer and the listener/reader. Faults in communication at these two levels are the results of bad language teaching, and can be remedied as language-learning problems. Faults at the semantic level of the communication, however, are less easy to identify. How far is this a matter of general education or general intelligence? How far does it lie within the scope of the language teacher? Grammatical systems have their own internal logic which a learner can master by understanding and patient practice. Semantics, however, presents different problems. Communication among native speakers of the same language most often breaks down at this point: 'What did he mean by that?' 'When you say "potential", do you mean . . . ?' 'Was he being sarcastic?' 'He doesn't understand what I'm getting at . . .' and so on.

It is doubtful whether all those semantic features peculiar to

English can be taught outside an English-speaking environment. It is debatable whether they can be taught in any complete way at all. We cannot know why we choose one method of expression rather than another, or the role of innate intelligence in such decisions. All we can do is increase our experience of words and their potential meanings, in order to have a wider range to choose from. There are basically two ways of doing this. Words have meaning because of their relationships to other words; they also have meaning as a result of their generally accepted referents. The first type of meaning can be taught by well-known techniques of 'improving your word-power'—such relationships as synonymy, antonymy, inclusion (flower—rose, violet), and so on, can all be employed. Exercises which require substitution of elements of the same word-class in sentences; exercises which link words together in meaning in the learner's mind; exercises which demonstrate such meanings by citing unambiguous examples: these are all legitimate means of increasing the learner's experience of words.

The second type of meaning which words possess involves relating them to contexts in which they may be used. This is largely a matter of choice of content—what we choose to use the language for when we teach it. The meaning of some items can be taught by simple demonstration, using real objects or pictures. But usually it will be necessary to supplement such demonstrations with a description, since different learners will have different perceptual problems. This is of particular importance in the use of television to teach meaning.

At this 'semantic' level of language acquisition, the receptive skills will be required to comprehend meaning beyond the recognition of the structures being employed. Material of increasing difficulty should be presented to the learner for him to extract information from it, and, later, to interpret it. As a listener, he will have to understand spoken directions or information, and interpret it according to his own needs. He will wish to understand the attitudes behind certain spoken expressions, and the style in which they are expressed. As a reader, he will want to find out information from written material of various kinds, and to interpret it in action (as in reading directions from a bottle of medicine). Exercises may be presented in interpreting various reports of the same event, to discover what actually occurred, and why each report is different. He may be asked to guess at the meaning of a written passage from a scrutiny of only the opening and closing paragraphs.

The productive skills, at the level of underlying meaning, need practice in expression: how to say what you mean with the language resources available to you. The work done on guided composition techniques is useful here. The learner-writer needs practice in controlled expression, with the gradual removal of structural and semantic controls. Another aspect of the semantic level of the writing skill is the art of the secretary—taking notes from read or heard material and putting them together in a complete form. Similar work needs to be done for the learner-speaker. He needs practice in creating spoken language from the short sentence to the longer description, or lecture. Students will be asked to talk about objects, films or events. Again, methods need to be devised to control this 'spoken composition' in the early stages, and gradually to remove the controls.

A Course Synthesis

Each skill, then, subsumes a variety of language functions at varying levels of difficulty. At each level, the four skills interrelate in such a way as to make their total separation in a teaching strategy out of the question. A synthesized course will need to bring in each skill as and when appropriate, at whatever level of difficulty is appropriate. The three levels of difficulty also interrelate: it is not possible to teach and practise the phonological and graphological realization of language satisfactorily without passing on to grammatical systems; meaning enters into the very first English language lesson. However, it seems likely that the first two years of an English course would teach and intensively practise the recognition and production of almost all the phonological and graphological features of English; that the basic structures of the simple English sentence would be taught and to some extent practised; and that a few exercises involving choices of meaning would be introduced, though there would be no systematic teaching of meaning as yet. Such a synthesis is, of course, speculative, and depends upon the age, mother-tongue, and education system of the learners. The synthesis should, ideally, be the result of a consideration of these various factors. It is based, however, upon an analysis of the second-language skills to be acquired and upon a continual awareness of the kind and degree of the learner's mental involvement in each operation.

We can now turn to the possible uses of television, basing our ideas upon this kind of language analysis. First, we need to go through each skill, at each level of difficulty, and to examine the kind of contribution which television might make. Later, a synthesis can be produced. Like the ELT course itself, the synthesized TV course will depend upon the age, mother-tongue and education system of the audience. If the audience is composed of home-viewing adults, one kind of synthesis will result; decisions will have to be made about the use of other elements, apart from TV, in the total teaching course. If the audience is composed of classroom students, following a centralized curriculum and text-book, a different synthesis may be necessary. To begin, however, we need an inventory of the possible uses of television in language teaching. We shall proceed on the lines laid out in the above analysis, taking each skill in turn, and progressing from the simplest to the more difficult components of each skill.

Note

Extensive use has been made of ideas expressed in *Blueprint for a Secondary English Course* by S. C. Murison-Bowie, 1969, mimeographed, a background paper to his *Contact: The Oxford Secondary English Course for Ethiopia*, Books 1 to 4, Oxford University Press 1970, 1972 and forthcoming.

5 Television and the Listening Skill

For an adequate control of the listening skill, the language learner needs to be able to recognize the range of segmental and supra-segmental features of English. He then needs repeated practice in these recognition techniques. How does television approach the problem of teaching and practising the phonological level of the listening skill? The first problem is an obvious one. Television operates in two modalities, sound and vision. A good deal of experimental work has been done on the relationship between these two in any communication.[1] One conclusion is that the success of the communication depends upon the degree of their integration. The sound and the pictures must complement each other. But if we are teaching recognition of sounds, we have to decide what the viewer is to look at. If this is simply a question of filling in one channel, the visual, with the least possible distractions, while communicating solely in the sound channel, then television should not handle this part of the language-teaching system.

Recognition of Sounds in Speech

For any particular phoneme in the English sound system, the learner requires to recognize it consistently, and to differentiate it from similar sounds. A large number of examples are required to enable him to do this. The teacher in the classroom can simply run through a large number of words which differ only in the particular phoneme he is teaching. Or else he can endeavour to make them meaningful by using words known to the student, or explaining those words he does not know. In teaching an initial *s/th* distinction, for example, he may run through *sink/think*, *sank/thank*, *sick/thick*, without exhausting the vocabulary of the students. He then has to test recognition, which can only be done by adopting the written or spoken mode. This procedure can be handled fairly simply by television. Television is the electronic embodiment of William James's dictum that 'the more other facts a fact is associated with in the mind, the better possession of it our memory retains'. Because of the resources available to television—film, studio, captions of all descriptions, electronic editing—it is possible to present a large number of examples of any one feature in a very short space of time. There are problems of television conventions which an audience may have to be taught. This is a topic to which we shall return later. But just as a classroom teacher, or a written set of exercises, takes a student through a whole range of conceptual jumps by presenting disconnected examples, so television can perform the same function much more efficiently, and with a much wider range of reference than is possible for the teacher. A teacher may have a struggle to find examples of an i/iː contrast, or an initial s/θ contrast within his classroom resources. It is for this reason that much speech practice is mere repetition, devoid of meaning for the learner. Television can make such speech practice meaningful by producing pictures in the visual mode, while giving the auditory information in the sound mode. There are limitations here too: the examples chosen have to be picturable, and as unambiguous as possible. This is a question of diagrammatic style, design conventions, and visual perception, which will be discussed in a later section. At this point it is enough to mention that connections between word and picture, however loosely presented, are acceptable to the learner for recognition purposes. Any teacher who has used stick figures on the blackboard to illustrate 'running' or 'climbing' will agree that it is the word-picture relation which matters, not the degree of exactitude of the relationship. It thus becomes possible to test a viewer-learner's recognition of sounds without requiring him to say the sounds himself, or to write down their graphological equivalents. Having presented a series of sound-picture relationships—*sink/think, sank/thank, sing/thing, sick/thick*, for example—recognition can be tested by reshowing one picture of each pair, with either the correct or incorrect sound form in the audio channel. The learner-viewer has then simply to say 'yes' or 'no', or to raise his hand when the correct sound-picture relationship is stated. His response can be checked immediately afterwards by giving the correct answer. It must be emphasized that the aim here is to make such speech practice meaningful, and that the process on television can be handled very speedily.

If the classroom teacher is not a native speaker of English, or where there is no teacher, television can be of use in the initial presentation of phonological material of this kind. How far it can be devoted to the intense practice of such material depends upon the length of television time available, and the other demands upon the medium in the total teaching course. If twenty minutes' television time per school day were allocated to just this element of the total course—recognition of the sounds of English—it would probably amount to more practice time than is devoted to the topic in the average English teaching class.

Intonation and Stress

The suprasegmental features of the English sound system lend themselves equally well to television treatment. Simple intonation patterns have been taught in the past by a variety of devices. A series of pictured, filmed, or studio examples can be used to accompany examples in the sound channel which carry the same tune: 'Is he sitting down?' 'Are they running away?' 'Is she making a dress?' and so on. Superimposed on the picture, the particular tune can be diagrammatically presented as a moving line, or series of dots. In one filmed ELT series, such a device has been used over written sentences; this brings in the reading skill when intonation is more properly the province of listening and speaking, and further complications are, perhaps, undesirable. In the listening skill, we are concerned that students recognize intonation patterns and what they convey. After sufficient practice, the learner-viewer can be asked to select right from wrong picture-sound relationships with regard to intonational contrasts, as with phonemic contrasts.

The teaching of the recognition of stress in English is probably more complicated. The question is whether a visual representation of stress patterns add anything to the information in the audio channel. However, the attention of the learner needs to be focused on weak and strong forms in English, especially if his mother-tongue is syllable-timed, and he is likely to transfer this system in his understanding of English. He may be confused by the difference in speed of delivery between the two sentences: 'My friend's father wore thick leather boots last week' and 'He would have been annoyed if he had known what people thought of him.' The stress in these two sentences is markedly different, and the learner-hearer needs to be made aware of the difference. It would probably be simpler if the sentences could be written down for demonstrative purposes. However, a useful demonstration would show a representation of the meaning of the sentence being spoken in the audio channel; a visual device could appear on the picture at the stress-points in the spoken sentence. Alternatively, the number of stress-points in the sentence might be visually tallied. When a particular stress-form has been sufficiently practised in this way, the learner-viewer could be required to check whether the visual stress-sign, or the stress-tally corresponds with the stress information in the audio channel.

Varieties of Speech

In the type of exercises suggested so far in the use of television for the teaching of the English sound system, much emphasis has been placed upon the use of pictures. That is, the recognition of heard sounds on a soundtrack, when the speaker himself is unseen. This is undoubtedly an important part of sound-recognition work since much listening material comes to us through radio, tapes, or conversations when we cannot see the speaker, watch his lip movements, and observe the gestures which help our understanding of his utterances. However, much can be learnt by seeing the speaker at close quarters. A classroom teacher who endeavours to demonstrate the position of the tongue for the English *l* in *lips*, or the lip positions for the vowel sounds in *lock/look* or *took/talk*, will find difficulty in demonstrating satisfactorily for the benefit of the whole class. Television can show the movements of the articulatory organs with great precision, either by close-ups of the speaker's mouth, or by filmed or diagrammatical representation of what happens to the organs of speech in particular functions. Such explanation could well accompany the recognition exercises mentioned earlier, since it helps understanding and consequently motivation. In teaching recognition of the sound system of English, it will be seen that a variety of techniques present themselves; among them, practice should be given in sounds from a seen speaker, and sounds from an unseen speaker.

It may be useful, in addition, to present varieties of spoken English to the learner-listener. This may be of particular concern where he is exposed to both English and American native speakers. There may well be difficulties where the sound systems of British and American English differ. Television presentation of such difficulties, contrasting an American and an English production of, for example, the vowel sounds in *last* or *box*, or differences in vowel length, or consonantal differences, such as the medial *t* in *water*, can provide a precise and rapid explanation. There is no need to dwell on such problems, since they tend to confuse the learner-listener. A short, one- or two-minute presentation of native speakers of the particular dialects, observed in surroundings typical of their own country, and heard to utter the same word in different ways, disposes of the problem efficiently. Apart from dialectal differences, there are other varieties of spoken English which the learner-listener may need to understand. Tone of voice normally distinguishes between formal and informal, but the expression of the speaker also helps to clarify the distinction. Learners may wish to recognize friendly from unfriendly intonation features in such simple structures as are often employed in classroom teaching situations. 'Go to the blackboard', 'Shut the door', and so on, can be said in different ways according to the attitude of the speaker. The listener will need to recognize such attitudes in the heard information, and a visual presentation of situations in which different styles are used can convey the point effectively.

Sound to Symbol

The sounds of English can often be recognized by their written form, and part of the listening skill may well involve the recognition of the relationships between sounds and written symbols. Instead of relating a picture in the video channel with the appropriate sound in the audio channel, it may be useful to substitute the printed word for the picture. Having presented, for example, *fill/feel, pill/peel, ship/sheep* in both video and audio channels, and practised them, recognition of the sound can be checked by presenting one of the pair on the screen, and either the right or wrong word in the audio channel, for the learner to recognize as correct or incorrect. Teaching might then progress to further presentation of such pairs as *bit/beat, lid/lead, mill/meal*, emphasizing the relationship of sound i: to spellings *ee* and *ea*, before continuing with recognition practice. If it is preferred to avoid the use of actual printed words, it may be thought advisable to teach the use of phonetic symbols and to use these in the same way. Stimulus pictures with the appropriate symbol being practised can be presented together with the correct word in the audio channel. Checking can then take the form of either relating sound to symbol, or relating symbol to picture. In the latter case, the viewer-learner has to recognize the pictured object, say the sound himself and check whether the phonetic symbol illustrated is the correct one.

Viewer Response

This last exercise raises the question of viewer response. In teaching the recognition of the sound system of English, response devices will vary according to the learner's ability in the productive skills. A variety of devices have already been suggested, in which the learner has to signify whether a sound-picture, or sound-word, or sound-symbol relationship is correct or incorrect. Further exercises might ask the learner to indicate whether two sounds are the same or different, or whether the initial consonant, say, in two pictured objects, is the same or different. If the audio channel is employed, the viewer's response will be a simple yes/no. If he is in a classroom with a teacher or monitor, he may be required to raise his hand for a correct response, so that the teacher can check. If he is a home learner, his response will remain internal. In both cases, the correct answer has to be given from the screen immediately afterwards. If the learner is learning to speak English, he may be asked to say 'yes' or 'no', 'correct' or 'incorrect', 'the same' or 'different'. If the learner is capable of a full spoken response, it will be possible to extend the recognition questions from a simple correct/incorrect system to a multiple-selection system. Then the learner-viewer can select from a series of alternatives by calling out the number of the correct answer.

In two exercises already mentioned the audio channel is not used; these are where a picture-phonetic sign relationship is used, and where two pictures are presented for the identification of, say, the initial consonant, or vowel sound appropriate to the pictured object. In both cases, the learner-viewer will have to say the name of the object or objects to himself before checking the sounds. For example, we may show a picture of a sheep and a picture of a car with a price tag indicating that it is very cheap. Having used both pictures in sound/picture practice, they may be produced again in a testing sequence, requiring the learner to say whether the initial consonants are the same or different. He will then have to produce *sheep* and *cheap* in order to answer. However incorrect his own production of the sounds in question, we shall still have tested his ability to recognize that they are different. If the viewer-learner's writing ability is adequate, he may be asked to write down the correct word for any given sound, or the correct phonetic symbol if these are to be taught.

One further point needs to be made here. All exercises depend upon a clear explanation to the learner-viewer of what is intended of him in the way of response. Practice has to be given, with sufficient examples, to enable him to answer the questions in the manner suggested. For each exercise, one system of response has to be maintained, or confusion will result. In sound recognition procedures, covert response is all that is required. An overt response may be required, however, by a teacher or monitor who is with a viewing class of students.

Recognition of Structures in Speech

In our discussion of the application of television to the listening skill, we can now move on to the next level of difficulty. The learner needs to recognize the grammatical arrangement of the data he hears, to understand the grammatical system in operation, and to apply this understanding to further data which he hears. We have to emphasize the syntactic information in the data, rather than the semantic information it carries. The material has to be presented to him in a graded form, with a sufficiently large number of examples of each item. He must be brought to an understanding of the particular structure in operation in the set of examples, and given more examples which practise his understanding of the use of the structure. A structure syllabus for the listening skill tends to correspond in the early years of language teaching to that of the speaking skill, and to be concerned with structures used in conversations. Later, other forms of listening material need to be incorporated: lectures, stories, play dialogues, where the speakers are seen, and radio and taped material where the speakers are unseen. Practice needs to be given, also, in training the listener to understand structures at only one hearing. All such material needs to be carefully written and selected, so that the semantic information causes no difficulty while we are practising and testing the structural information the material contains.

One of the problems of language-teaching method, which has carried over to ELT television programmes, is largely concerned with the demonstrability of certain structures. Just as in television news coverage, there is little point in reporting something which cannot be illustrated, so structure syllabuses for ELT tend to be based upon a principle of ease of demonstration. We can picture a man running and say 'the man is running'. It is less simple to picture 'Let's go for a swim', or 'He doesn't go to work everyday'. Partly this is a matter of conventions, mentioned earlier. Many teachers will differentiate between *this* and *that*, by touching an object in the first case, and pointing to a more distant object in the second—an artificial convention which does not, perhaps, reflect the actual use of these two words. A convention is used for the purposes of exposition. Similar conventions can be used for a large number of structures in the syllabus. To ensure real understanding, however, it may be necessary to use other means—explanation, translation, and so on. Having established a firm understanding of the structure, it becomes necessary to drill it in a wide variety of examples.

In teaching and practising each particular structure in the syllabus, we have to talk about something. A teacher may use the classroom situation, or use pictures to give the students a semantic framework within which to practise a particular structure. He will certainly move randomly from one concept to another, within such a framework: the linking factor will be the structure itself. Flexibility in his choice of semantic content is essential if he is to provide examples of the structure he is teaching in sufficient abundance. A television programme also has to present material in such a way as to provide a lot of examples of the same structure. Otherwise, there can be no learning and no practice. It is here that the conventional 'situational English' television programme falls down. It presents 'real' situations which use examples of structural items from a graded syllabus. The more 'real' it attempts to be, the less possible it becomes to fit examples of the particular structure into the script in any useful quantity. If the script begins from the premise of the structure itself, the situation becomes artificial to the point of absurdity. There are two further objections to this type of presentation of structural material. The dramatization of material in itself does not increase learning, as various experiments have shown. In language learning, particularly, dramatization of material intended to teach and practise recognition of structure can only serve as a distraction from the purpose in hand. Further, when attempting to check the learner's ability to recognize the structures which have been used in the situation, there are problems of memory retention. The learner has to be reminded of the use of the structure in the situation before it can be tested. 'Situational' presentation of structures has a place in practising the listening skill, but at a fairly advanced stage. By definition, the 'situation' has to do with extra-linguistic factors as much as the language that is used in it. The understanding of it, therefore, has much more to do with the meaning plane of language learning, than the structural plane.

An alternative would be to present structures for recognition as the teacher does in the classroom; to have a presenter-teacher who demonstrates 'I'm opening the box. I'm closing the box.' 'The book which is on the table is thick. The book which is on the chair is thin', and so on. Such a procedure is perfectly acceptable, if unexciting. Much depends upon the quality of the teachers in the education system in which the television is being used, and other factors in the total teaching system.

An extension of this practice is a little more interesting. Just as the teacher produces a wide range of examples to illustrate the same item, so television can utilize its visual eclecticism to perform the same function more efficiently. Whereas the teacher has to set up his examples in a classroom, and is limited by the classroom materials available to him, television can jump from one example to the next very rapidly, and use a wider frame of semantic reference. Let us look at a few examples. In the first or second year of English, the present simple tense may occur in the structure syllabus, and learners will need to recognize it. It will be necessary to explain the meaning of *everyday* and confirm that it is understood. Then a whole range of examples can be presented in the audio channel to the accompaniment of still pictures or film in the video channel: wakes up, gets up, washes, cleans, brushes, puts on, eats, drinks, goes . . . and so on. The same set of actions can equally well demonstrate the simple past tense, having established an understanding of *yesterday, last week,* or other time phrases. The use of the word *ago* with the simple past tense can be demonstrated by relating past actions to the present, intercutting the actions with a clock face, or a calendar, to indicate how long ago the action took place. The use of a structural item such as 'Let's . . .' is demonstrable on television by a series of paired stills or filmed shots, in 'before and after' fashion: people looking hot/ 'Let's have a drink'/people drinking; people carrying a heavy box/'Let's put it down'/box on the ground; people looking at a map/'Let's ask the way'/people asking someone who points in the direction they should take, and so on. The use of 'may' can be shown by following someone along a street with a camera, and asking 'What is she going to do?'. She may turn left . . . no, she hasn't. She may cross the street . . . yes, she's crossed the street. She may buy some vegetables . . . no, she's bought some fruit.

These visual presentations of examples of structure do not teach in themselves. There is no watertight structure-to-situation relationship. The presentation of examples this way does two things. First, it presents the structure which is to be taught. The teaching can then refer to these examples to explain the structure and its use; and understanding may be achieved inductively or deductively, by explanation or, perhaps, translation. Second, the examples give practice in recognition of the structure which has been taught. At a later stage, they enable the learner to apply his understanding to new material. Television's great asset in this area is the speed with which it can present a large number of examples to assist learning. Having established a pattern, such as 'He was/They were/taken to the airport', it is possible to employ visual substitutions for *taken* and *airport*, such as 'invited/driven/flown/pushed/pulled/shown' and 'garage/town/village/shop/farm' and so on. In this way, the learner is presented with a rapid series of new contexts in which the structure he is learning is used. He has to apply his understanding of the structure to each example.

The question follows of the learner-viewer's response by which he may check his progress. As with phonological material for listening and recognition, responses may be covert or overt. Whichever it is, the response has to monitor the learner's understanding of the structure, and not the meaning it embodies. Having established structure-picture relationships in presentation and practice work, the same relationships can be tested by varying correct and incorrect connections between the audio channel (structure) and the video channel (context). The learner will have to recognize correct from incorrect relationships, and his decision will be checked immediately afterwards. For example, two or three people are pictured going into a cinema, and the audio channel conveys, '*She* is going to the cinema.' The learner has to recognize the lack of pluralization. The correct picture-structure relationship would have been demonstrated in presentation and practice work. Similarly, in a lesson which had differentiated between *may* and *must*, a picture might show a car at a red traffic-light, while the audio channel gives the sentence, 'You may stop at a red light.' Again, the learner-viewer would be expected to recognize the wrong use of *may*. A further covert response might be the presentation of multiple answers from which the learner has to select one correct one. Difficult to do orally, because of the memory retention factor, such a covert response is only feasible where the learner can also read. He can then be asked to pick out the number of the correct answer. Alternatively, the screen could be divided into four sections, either on a still caption, or on film, or electronically, to present four alternatives for one structure in the audio channel. The viewer-learner has then to select the picture which corresponds with the structure he hears. For example, the heard structure, 'He's been pushed into the water', could also be pictured, together with pictures illustrating, 'He'll be pushed', 'He's being pushed', 'He pushed someone'. Such checking procedures would, again, follow presentation of the structure-picture relationship in presentation or practice work.

Overt tests of recognition of heard structures will vary according to the speaking ability achieved by the learner. He may be required to answer, 'Yes, he is', or 'No, he isn't', and so on. A picture showing a man on the edge of a lake, with the structure, 'Has he been pushed in the water?' will elicit the response, 'No, he hasn't'. At a later stage, questions beginning with question-words may be asked. Care must be taken to make sure the learner-viewer knows exactly what kind of reply is expected from him. At this stage, we are concerned with structure-recognition, and not structure-production. 'How long ago did they leave?' in the audio channel, with the answer illustrated, would expect the answer 'Ten minutes', etc., rather than 'They left ten minutes ago'. An oral 'fill-in-the-blank' system is possible; with the appropriate picture, the audio channel might convey, 'He . . . in the water this morning', and ask the learner-viewer to say the correct form of the word. If the reading and writing skills are sufficiently developed, written fill-in-the-blank forms may be used on the screen, asking the learner-viewer either to say the missing word, or else to write it down.

As with exercises in sound recognition, these structure-recognition exercises depend upon a clear exposition of what is required from the learner. The answering conventions must be clearly established with sufficient examples, and such conventions should not change their form without further examples being given. Because of the medium's facility in rapidly presenting a large amount of material, such explanatory examples will not take a great deal of time, and will ensure the success of the following exercises.

Understanding Meaning in Speech

We have now looked at teaching the recognition of the sounds and structure of speech—or the coding systems of heard information. Structure cannot be taught without some reference to the meaning of the words which the structure uses. Meaning will be taught from the early lessons of English: classroom objects, action words, and so on. But beyond the presentation of those words which are required to fill out the teaching of structure, little attempt is made systematically to teach language meaning as such. As mentioned earlier, this is divisible into the internal meaning of words—the meaning relations which exist between words; and the external meaning of words which is derivable from the context in which they are used.[2]

Word Relationships

The teaching of word meanings in early stages may be done by grouping them together in some convenient way, and grading the conceptual difficulty of the meaning relations[3] which exist between the words in any one group. If teaching by means of inclusion groups, *apple, orange, lemon, plum, chair* may be presented to begin with; later, *potato* might be substituted for *chair*; later still *strawberry* for *potato*. With each change, the definition of the inclusion group would change, from 'things to eat' to 'fruit', to 'fruit growing on trees'. Similarly, the list, *skirt, dress, shoes, blouse, umbrella* could be followed by *shoelace* being substituted for *umbrella*, then *trousers* for *shoelace*. In each case, the learner has to redefine more and more closely the meaning-relationship which holds the group. Other types of groupings are possible. Having presented the word *dry*, students can be asked which of a list is most like the given word in meaning—*long, heavy, tired, blue, wet*. Or, given the word *washing*, the list might be, *reading, cleaning, wearing, setting*. Such lists can be presented rapidly in visual form on television. At this stage of language learning, the student probably has some command of written English, in which case the list of words can be superimposed in order at the side of the screen as each picture is shown. Film, or studio presentation might be employed to demonstrate such relationships as exist between *become—be, get—have, offer—accept/refuse* and so on.

Apart from showing meaning-relationships between words in a group, techniques of definition and inference are also common methods of teaching meaning. An object, action or event may be shown in such a way as to be unclear—perhaps shot from a strange angle, shown in big close-up, or defocused. The audio channel can define or describe the object, and leave time for the viewer to guess its meaning before the camera zooms out, refocuses, or shoots it from a different angle to demonstrate its meaning clearly. Alternatively, two or three pictures may be shown, a definition or description given in the audio channel, and the viewer-learner asked to select the picture which fits the definition or description. Such procedures involve careful, unambiguous writing.

Exercises in word groups may be eclectic to the point of selecting any examples for the purpose of the grouping to be practised. It is more likely, however, that the words will evolve from other parts of the total television programme. This will be discussed when we come to talk about the synthesis of the various language skills. It is important, however, to include practice in the understanding of word-meanings in connected passages. Such material has to be carefully written so that it includes techniques to help the listener to understand. Definitions may be written into the passages, or the particular word may be described in words familiar to the learner. At the same time, the listener needs to understand different types of subject-matter, different styles of speech, and different methods of speech presentation.

Content

In subject-matter, a school educational television system may be interested in the presentation of material from other subject areas in the language programmes. Scientific material, commentary on experiments, geographical descriptions, and so forth, may all be used as content material for listening comprehension. A general audience will need to understand current-affairs material, spoken recipes or handy hints for home-proud husbands, directions for going places and doing things, general information, entertainment material, and so on. The understanding of speech style is also important—the formal newsreader and the informal discussion of information between two friends. A guide might formally describe the contents of a stately home, or a museum; one of the tourists might then be shown taking a friend over the same material, but in an informal style. A programme might show someone asking for information, asking for help, requesting the return of a spade his neighbour has borrowed: the same material can be demonstrated in both formal and informal styles to show the difference in approach. It is at this level of 'language in context' that the television is of obvious value. It is a duplication of its function in the entertainment field. The difference is that the ELT programme grades its material and draws the viewer's attention to what is being taught.

We hear spoken information in a variety of ways, and learners will need to understand speech in these various modes. There is the face-to-face mode, as is encountered in the lecture, or the film. Material needs to be written into lecture form, dialogue form, interview form. Plays and sketches are all useful, as are studio interviews and filmed interviews with people engaged in a particular occupation, or stopped in the street and asked their opinion. Again, the material has to be carefully prepared and rehearsed for maximum understanding. It may incorporate features of other language skills being taught in the programme; this is, again, a matter for programme synthesis. In this mode of presentation, the speakers are always visible to the listeners. A second mode which requires practice is the studio demonstration-description. In this mode, the speaker talks to the camera, or to someone else in the studio, and refers to objects, pictures, charts, graphs. The speaker directs the listener's attention to features of these visual aids while he is talking about them. Lastly, there is the commentary mode, where the speaker is never seen. Particular attention has to be paid here to the relation between the sound and visual channels of communication. One cannot talk about Rembrandt while showing pictures of a power-station, and hope that both channels will communicate effectively to the listener-viewer. Films which show wildlife or current events, general interest films, or films about other subjects in the curriculum, may all be used for this purpose, so long as the soundtrack corresponds to the pictures seen, and is graded to suit the ability of the listener. At an advanced stage of listening and understanding practice, it may be possible to relate picture and sound in a more interesting manner so that they do not correspond. A film of a lavish home and life-style may be shown to the accompaniment of a commentary complaining about the poverty of the inhabitants; shots of children playing on a climbing-frame may be accompanied by a commentary which attacks the inhuman physical tortures which schoolchildren are exposed to. Such techniques are used more and more in film and television work, and are used to make a point. In teaching a listening skill, they should be used with circumspection, and only for a clear purpose—that of asking the learner-listener to correctly interpret the information he receives. Such exercises are important if the learner is to understand, not only modern film and television devices, but also such speech features as sarcasm, cynicism, humour and lying.

In testing the semantic level of the listening skill, we are less concerned with the correct recognition of structure than the correct understanding of the underlying information or implication of material presented to the ear. In early stages, comprehension should aim at extracting information from heard material. Factors such as the length of the passage and retrievability of the information will affect student performance. It may be preferred on occasion to ask questions before the presentation of the material, so that the student listens, looking for a particular piece of information. If the questions are asked afterwards, they may be simple true-false type, or presented in a written multiple-choice form. It may be necessary to repeat material for listening more than once, to assist comprehension. This should not be relied upon, however, since the listener has to accustom himself to a single exposure to most material he hears. At a more advanced level, comprehension questions should aim at the interpretation of heard information. Playlets and interviews are of particular value here. Learners should be encouraged to understand, not only what the speaker says, but why he says it, and what interpretation therefore has to be put upon the information. A simple example might be five or six different opinions about a traffic accident, given by the people involved. Television excels in this kind of presentation. Since the 'television election' in Britain in 1959, both politicians and viewers have had to come to terms with the medium's ability faithfully to present, or unfaithfully to distort, the truth.[4] There is no question of 'manipulation' here; the listener has to evaluate critically what he hears. And it is part of a language course to train him to do just this.

Notes

1. Graeme Kemelfield: 'Progress Report of the Schools Television Research Project' (Leeds) Part II in *E.T.I.* Vol. 3 No. 3
2. S. Pit Corder: 'The Teaching of Meaning' in *Applied Linguistics and the Teaching of English* (eds. Hugh Fraser and W. R. O'Donell) Longmans 1969
3. For an account of meaning relations see John Lyons: *An Introduction to Theoretical Linguistics* Cambridge University Press 1968, chapter 10
4. Joseph Trenaman and Denis McQuail: *Television and the Political Image* Methuen 1961

6 Television and the Speaking Skill

The television medium is most obviously suited to the receptive skills, there is no doubt. Watching any television programme itself involves a receptive ability on the part of the viewer, to understand what he sees and hears. Commercial television is constantly fighting to capture and retain the viewer's passive interest. Even popular quiz programmes make things easy for the viewer by using a studio panel to do the thinking work for them. Yet television does have the potential to involve the viewer to a much greater extent, to engage his interest to the point where his participation becomes active. The viewer may be sufficiently interested to fetch pencil and paper and write down a recipe. Where he is not viewing alone, he may feel the need to compete in a quiz programme with other viewers in front of the same receiver, and answer questions vocally. Ray Bradbury, in his story, *Fahrenheit 451* imagines the excitement of a housewife who is actually allowed to take a role in a television drama; the screen character turns to the camera and says, 'What do you think?' and the housewife says her lines, which have been sent to her through the post.[1]

Problems of Viewer Participation

In the Bradbury story, it was necessary to use another medium—print—to get the housewife to participate. In a number of ELT television programmes, the accompanying textbook, records or tapes have been the sole means of ensuring audience involvement to the point where they will speak English. Television has tended to assume the worst: unmotivated students who will only demonstrate their motivation by the purchase of ancillary material; or a general audience unwilling to speak out to an inanimate television screen in their own home. Recognition procedures as are involved in the receptive skills allow the viewer-learner to participate without embarrassment, and to test himself without showing his failure or success.

The non-captive viewer-learner, his individual viewing environment and feelings have to be considered. Some members of such an audience will respond to a screen, just as children do, when asked, 'Are you sitting comfortably?'. But this assumption cannot be made. The most that can be done is to allow time for viewer response, which may or may not be utilized. The result, for most ELT television programmes for general audiences, has been an unwillingness to spend a great deal of time on the speaking skill. The bulk of television time has been taken up with the presentation of 'language in context', presumably for recognition purposes; the audience has then been encouraged to say those structures which it has heard. Sometimes this has been simple imitation; sometimes it has involved the production of a structure which fits a situation which the viewer observes; sometimes it has involved the transformation of one read or heard structure into another which the viewer has to produce. Such exercises, however, have taken up a small proportion of the available airtime.

Apart from the problems raised by the non-captive learner himself—his motivation, learning environment and so on—there are two pedagogical arguments which militate against extending the teaching of speech on television. First, it is impossible to monitor each student's production of the language, to check where each is making an error and to initiate remedial action. It can be counter-argued that this is not an important objection; the statistical justification of the objective language test is that the ability to distinguish right from wrong structures is closely correlated with the ability to produce right from wrong structures. But this refers to an understanding of structure. It may apply to the grammatical and semantic levels of the language skills, but not to the phonology of a language. Many students may be able to hear, and then produce what they hear accurately. But experience indicates that this is far from being the general rule, especially in those cases where sounds, stress and intonation patterns exist in the second language but not in the learner's mother-tongue. This objection applies to any medium the learner may use—radio, TV, tapes, records—where there is no native-speaker of the second language to check the learner's responses.

The second pedagogical factor is the amount of practice which the learner requires to make his speech production automatic. This applies to the phonological, structural and semantic level of spoken language. Ancillary material in the form of records and tapes can alleviate this problem, though without the constant check on the learner's response which the classroom teacher provides it is an open question how much such practice is worth. Even if an educational television system allowed one hour per day in the teaching and practice of spoken English, there would be no way of knowing how far the non-captive learner would benefit from such practice. Bearing in mind the environmental and motivational problems of the learner, and the absence of any response checking procedures, it is unlikely that any ETV organization would put out such quantities of spoken practice material, even if the airtime were available.

How far do these objections apply to the supervised learner, who watches television programmes in the company of an English language teacher or monitor? Being captive within a system, learner factors of motivation and embarrassment are less important; they are not the responsibility, at least, of the television producer. So far as attracting an audience is concerned, it is the teacher who has to be wooed; it is enough that he understands where the television programmes fit into his total teaching scheme and what his role has to be during a television lesson. But what of the two pedagogical objections to the teaching of speech on television—checking learner response, and degree of practice? Where the classroom teacher is a native-speaker of English, the checking of responses can be left to him. During a television drill, he can discover which of his pupils are accurately producing the model utterance given by the TV teacher, and which pupils require correction and special attention. In closed-circuit, or limited open-network TV operations, it may be possible to go off the air for a few minutes during a programme, to enable the teacher to carry out the kind of corrective work which is necessary. Where this is not possible, the teacher has to reserve his corrective procedures until the TV programme is finished. The classroom teacher who is not a native-speaker of English is a different problem. Everything depends upon his own ability in the productive skills of English, and how far he is able accurately to produce a model utterance presented by a TV teacher. This is, strictly speaking, a teacher-training problem, and there is very little that ELT television programmes can do to help it.

As far as practice procedures are concerned, the existence of a teacher or monitor, whether a native-speaker of English or not, makes things much easier for the television producer. The time given to speech practice will still depend upon extra-linguistic factors: airtime, the type of course synthesis, and so on. But procedures for drilling speech from a television screen are simpler where there is a teacher who is briefed as to the role he has to play. We will discuss the various types of drill when we come to elaborate the different levels of the speech skill. At this point we will mention the conventions of speech practice which are possible from a TV screen. Speech production may be a matter of simple repetition, either of single sounds, words, or whole sentences. The practice devices available to the classroom teacher are here available to the television producer. He may ask for a choral response from the whole viewing class; he may ask for group response within the class, or for individual response. A cue system is needed for these procedures; if the teacher is on camera, he may gesture to the camera to begin the viewers' response by pointing, or cupping his hand to his ear; there may be visual cues in the form of a graphic symbol, or there may be a sound cue. The cueing system has to be communicated to the viewers, either from the screen, or in accompanying material. The teacher in the classroom may have to reinforce the cueing system, by using his own gestures. If group, or individual response is required, arrangements have to be made, either from the screen, or in the ancillary notes, for the teacher to divide the class into groups when asked to do so, or to select individuals for responses when appropriate. One such system is to ask the teacher to allot numbers to the students; a television presenter then asks for a response from a particular number.[2] Timing of responses is also important; space left for viewer response should be neither too long nor too short. Some presenters mouth, or whisper the response to keep the viewers together. In repetition of pattern drills, however, the stress features should be sufficiently prominent in the model for the viewers to pick it up naturally in their response. With the teacher standing near the television set during such drills, to encourage, to beat out stress patterns and to monitor individual response for later correction, it is possible to conduct television drills in the same fashion as classroom drills.

Problems arise when students are required to do more than repeat after a television presenter. Substitution drills of varying complexity will involve a certain amount of thought on the part of the viewers before they respond. Experience indicates that sound substitutions are more readily grasped than visual substitutions. For example, if the lesson was practising 'I met my brother at the airport', and substituting other phrases for 'at the airport', viewer response is faster if the substitutions are presented orally: 'in the garage/at home/at school/in the street'. If such phrases had been presented for teaching purposes in visual form—photographs or drawings—subsequent practice may wish to employ the same visual stimuli. Response will then be delayed, since the viewers will have to recognize the picture, select the correct item and produce it. If the picture-response relationship has been sufficiently well established in the presentation stage, then practice responses may well be automatic. But where substitutions are being used to help the student to create language—to build upon his knowledge of a structure and produce new sentences—then response will perforce be more hesitant.

Speech practice by television is therefore possible, in terms of the kind of practice conventions available. It is unlikely, however, that television would ever be called upon to provide the total range of spoken practice material which a learner needs. It is also impossible to provide the instant monitoring system on individual learner's responses which the classroom teacher can provide. Approximations can be made, where the learners are viewing with a native-speaker of English. But generally speaking, television speech practice has to assume a learner's ability to produce correctly the sounds and structures that he hears. Given these limitations, we can go on to discuss where television might be of assistance in helping a learner to produce spoken language at the three levels of phonology, structure and meaning.

Production of Speech Sounds

The learner's production of the sounds of English is closely tied to his ability to recognize them correctly. But whereas television can present sounds for recognition exercises with great rapidity, and the viewer-learner may be expected to keep up with the speed, production of the same sounds involves slow and patient practice. However, the range of sound contrasts which the learner has to produce is probably more limited than the range he will have to learn to recognize. Neither receptive nor productive skills can be based upon a fixed sound system—a set of sounds each having an absolute form. The learner will have to understand many varieties of English, including that variety spoken by other speakers of his own mother-tongue. It is a waste of time to train him to produce these different varieties, and the allophonic differentiations they make. This is not to imply, however, that 'so long as he is intelligible', any crude approximation to the English sound-system will do. The learner has to be able to make the full range of phonemic contrasts in English, even if the relative values of such contrasts differ from those of an English or American native-speaker. The teaching of the system will depend upon the sound features of the mother-tongue. Certain sounds of English which do not exist in the mother-tongue will require particular practice, though decisions will have to be made concerning acceptable allophonic variants. Distribution features may require practice—unfamiliar consonant clusters which may not exist in the mother-tongue in the initial or final position, as in English. A television presentation can present a model of each sound, show the articulatory movements which produce it, explain its production in terms of the nearest equivalent in the learner's mother-tongue. The sound can then be contrasted with other sounds in English, and such contrasts contextualized by the use of paired words. Students might be asked to use mirrors to observe lip movements or tongue position in their own performance of the sound concerned. At each stage in this presentation, the viewer-learner has to be exhorted to repeat the model presented, or to go through the steps which lead to its production. Léon suggests, for example, that the final sound in the French word *paille*, might be taught from the point of view of the English *a/yes*; the final *s* is dropped, the *e* shortened, until the *aille* sound is produced.[3] If such a procedure were adopted for a television presentation, we would demonstrate the target sound, identify it from contexts, explain it in terms of the learner's mother-tongue, demonstrate articulatory movements involved, and then drill it from the *a/yes* form by means of demonstration and viewer response. A similar procedure may be usable for certain sounds in the English system. In subsequent practice sessions, it would be necessary to present the sound in minimal pair contrasts, and drill the viewers in producing such contrasts. Further practice may be done by the judicious selection of verses or songs which demonstrate the sound contrast under discussion. At a later stage still, the visual element of television might be brought into its own by visualizing minimal pairs, as was discussed in relation to the listening skill. This time, however, the emphasis would be upon response. For example, the pictured sequence might run, *cat/cart, hat/heart, back/bark, ladder/larder.* Having presented the pictures and sounds for response, the pictures might be presented by themselves, the viewers asked to say the correct word, and their pronunciation checked immediately afterwards. Songs and rhymes can also be pictured, and also such useful absurdities as 'Thirty-three thin thieves', 'The waiter gave the lady eight grey cakes', 'The straw is too strong to stretch', and so on. All these are useful devices for producing imitated responses; the use of pictures provides the unspoken stimulus for further practice.

Intonation and Stress

Suprasegmental features of English phonology are so diverse that the bulk of them probably fall into that category of language items which are only naturally produced by a non-English speaker after prolonged exposure to an English-speaking environment. The structural and semantic levels of language activity are increasingly important here, since both determine the selection of intonation and stress patterns. When learning the listening skill, the ability to decode the suprasegmental features, the learner can be presented with a selected range, he can be taught their significance, and he can practise his skill in decoding them. When it comes to producing them, however, the problem is more complex. The learner-listener can wait for a complete utterance and decode it. The learner-speaker has to initiate the utterance. The evidence suggests that we plan our speech segments in 'tone-groups'—an utterance of about seven or eight syllables, which has only one syllable with major prominence. This syllable tends to appear towards the end of the tone-group, but it dictates the way we say the rest of the utterance preceding the prominent syllable. Thus, the speaker thinks what he wants to say, plans the way he says it, and then says it.[4] The learner-speaker, therefore, has to achieve the automaticity of this speech act. The closed systems of sound and structure can be taught him and practised; the full range of intonation and stress elements relate more directly to the initial level of the speech act, where the idea to be communicated is formed. Only a very restricted range of items can be taught with any hope that they will be learnt, practised and applied to further material. There are two dangers in this type of instruction: first, that the restricted range selected will be over-emphasized (one criticism made of a BBC series was the 'most unusual intonation patterns in a beginner's course';[5] what is a 'usual' intonation pattern?); second, that any attempt to grade a course in English intonation will probably be contradicted every time the teacher opens his mouth. For example, a teacher may ask one student, 'What am I doing?' with a falling intonation; when he asks the same question to a second student, for practice purposes, it will be hard for him to avoid using a rising intonation. There are a vast number of situational and emotional conditions to the suprasegmental features we choose to use; for the native-speaker, such conditions affect the ideation stage of language production. The second-language learner can only acquire such flexibility when his utterances are mentally initiated and planned with the automaticity of the native-speaker.

In sum, the teaching of the production of suprasegmental elements must rely upon hearing and imitating; the learner will not be able to deduce any general rules from such a method, which he might apply with safety to further material. Even a basic division of tone patterns into 'Tune 1 and Tune 2' can be contradicted by any number of examples. The best we can do is to present material in such a way as to indicate that 'tones of voice' help to convey an impression we would like to give. For example, a parameter might be employed such as: politeness, friendliness, formality, unpleasantness, rudeness. The same utterance—'Give me that book', 'What is your name?'—can be presented for imitation according to each point on the parameter. Television can demonstrate this simply and easily by means of film, and the responses can be practised later by means of still pictures, or drawings, indicating the type of impression to be conveyed. Apart from this, the production of suprasegmental features has to derive from the imitation of models, and must rely upon the ability of the learner to reflect them accurately. Such practice forms a natural part of the structural and semantic levels of the speaking skill. In addition, practice may be given in the form of constructed dialogues which employ a particular intonation or stress feature. A short filmed or televised sketch may frame a dialogue such as:

A. Do you want this dress?
B. I think I prefer that one.
A. But that isn't nearly as pretty as this one.
B. I think that one suits me much better.

The features of stress and intonation embodied in such a dialogue can be repeated by a viewer. After he has heard the text once or twice, he may be asked to speak first A's lines, and then B's lines. The learner should be encouraged to say the words in the same way as the model. The words should not be written down for the learner in the ancillary material, since the fact of reading will distort his imitation of the correct pattern. Such a technique is the same as that mentioned in the Ray Bradbury story referred to at the beginning of this section. As a means of teaching intonation and stress as an end in itself, however, the method can do very little; it can only touch upon the range of expression which is available to the native-speaker. The very fact that the intonation and stress patterns mould structured dialogue polarizes Abercrombie's distinction between 'spoken prose' and real conversation even more.[6] The artificiality of what we teach has to be particularly borne in mind when we approach the problem of the suprasegmental features of speech.

Production of Structures in Speech

The production of the grammatical forms of English in speech is closely related to the ability to recognize such forms. For both, a graded sequence of structures has to be produced, and it tends to be the same for both. The learners need to be presented with examples of spoken structures, they need to be brought to an understanding of the operative system in a particular utterance, and they need to be presented with opportunities to apply their understanding in the production of further utterances based upon the same system. Speech in these circumstances is, of course, artificially produced, in the sense that the stimulus for speech is given to the student. At the later, semantic, level of speech function, we shall have to discuss the question of the ideation stage of speech production. Here, we are concerned that the student may have the facility to speak in acceptable grammatical forms, so that when he eventually 'creates' speech from initial idea to phonological realization, he has the language tools to carry it out successfully. When we teach and practise an ability to produce grammatically correct utterances, it is necessary to provide the student with the stimulus for speech.

This means providing a number of contexts in which may occur the speech activity which employs the particular structure we are interested in at any one time. All this means is the provision of something to use the structure for—something to talk about. The context we provide may be as short as a single utterance, or a longer, 'situational' context. But the context has to be simple, requiring no thought on the part of the student. The meaning has to be quite clear, since the emphasis is on the structural framework of the context; any context which distracts from this because thought is required to comprehend it, can only serve to interfere with the learning process at this stage. In presenting a series of stimuli for producing the same grammatical structure, it should be possible for the student to leap mentally from one to the next without hesitation. Thus: 'While he was in the bath, the telephone rang', may be followed immediately by, 'While he was at work, his house caught fire'. There is no need for a television script to set up a single elaborate situation in which a structure can be used many times. It is more efficient to use television's voracious appetite for information, by presenting a large number of short contexts as stimuli for speech by the learner.

These contexts may be put together into exercises, employing live studio action, short film excerpts, animation, still photographs, or drawings, or various combinations of these visual sources. At the simplest level, the viewer-learner may be required only to respond as to structure recognition exercises: 'Yes/No/Yes it is/No he doesn't', and so on. Or he may be asked simply to repeat structures which he hears on the sound channel while viewing related pictures; the sound stimulus will then be removed, and the learner has then to produce the structure associated with the picture directly. Techniques of response have already been discussed. Stress plays an important part in attempting to control the speed and manner of response, but the longer the utterance, the more difficult this becomes. A variant of the simple repetition exercise is to ask the viewer-learner to complete and repeat sentences in which gaps have been left: 'When did he go to the village? He ——————— to the village yesterday.'

The most satisfactory type of repetition drills are those where the question and reply are equally well structured, and where the viewer-learner can be 'conditioned' to provide either. 'When's he going to finish his homework?/He's just finished it': 'When's he going to see the film?/He's just seen it': 'When's he going to read that book?/He's just read it'.[7] Such a sequence can be easily illustrated; viewer-learners can initially listen to examples of the exchange, then give the replies each time. Later they can be asked to say the question form whenever the appropriate picture is shown. Structured dialogues mentioned earlier in connection with the practice of spoken intonation patterns, are also useful for practising spoken structures. A short exchange between two characters can be shown several times; the viewer can then be asked to say the lines of one of the characters and then the lines of the other.

In order to encourage the student to build upon his understanding of spoken structures, some form of substitution exercise is necessary. If the basic pattern, 'Has/Have she/they done something?' has been demonstrated and practised in repetition drills, it may be useful to allow the student to expand on this. 'Has/Have the hunters/they/she/the fat man/the people

caught/bought/brought/taken/eaten a fish/deer/rabbit/duck?'
By substituting words in one section of the structure, and keeping
the rest constant, the student can be asked to say a variety of
sentences as a series of pictures are shown, each one relating to
the substitution the speaker has to make. The main problem connected with this type of exercise is the selection of substitute words
the speaker is asked to say. It is not always possible to know what
words he may have already met.

Practice such as this, at the phonological and structural levels of
the speaking skill, is a dreary business in the most scintillating
classroom. It is a slow process, and is not helped by the artificial
nature of the material and the enforced method of its presentation. When these drills are conducted by television a great deal of
time is spent in setting up the stimulus-response patterns. The
writing of the drills so as to obtain the precise response required is
a difficult art, and tends to exclude a great deal of material which
requires practice, but which cannot be unambiguously presented
in drill form. In addition, there are the enormous problems attendant upon regulating response to a television screen from a single
home viewer and from a student in a classroom. If these problems
can be overcome, and if the response patterns can be fixed in the
students' minds so that they adjust rapidly to them, then speech
practice is a possibility through the medium of television. The
intensity of the practice depends upon airtime available; speech
drills for an hour per school day would undoubtedly do some
good. Only by this kind of intensity of practice can the speech
patterns be sufficiently well-established in the learner's mind to be
automatically available to him when he wishes to express an idea
in speech.

Saying what you Mean to Say

Between the idea and the structural and phonological expression
of it, there is likely to be a two-way relationship. While the idea
conditions the structures and sounds we employ, these language
'tools' also affect the formulation of the idea, the way of express-
ing it, and therefore the intention behind it. For the native-
speaker, such a two-way relationship is complex because he has a

greater range of ability in the language skills with which to frame an idea he wishes to express. For the second-language learner, similarly, the extent of his skill in using the systems of the language will affect, not only the expression of ideas, but also their formulation. Subtle argument may be beyond his powers until he has studied a language for several years; meanwhile, his arguments will necessarily be simplistic or else badly expressed. In teaching the spoken skill, it is important to train the learner to express ideas with the language skills available to him at any particular moment. The techniques of guided written composition are relevant here. To create, or initiate language, the idea to be expressed has to be controlled within the known grammatical grasp and fluency of the learner. When practising the production of grammatical systems in speech, this control is absolute. As we have discussed, the stimuli for speech in this practice is provided for the learner; no idea-formulation is required from him. He simply repeats, or, at most, substitutes known words in the structure. His mental activity is confined to the manipulation of the structure he is practising. As we come to the 'semantic' level of speech production, however, this type of control has to be gradually relaxed, in proportion to the increased fluency of the learner in the grammatical systems of language.

At the most controlled level of oral expression, we may simply extend a practice used for teaching structure. One particular structure is used in a series of sequential sentences, which, together, make up a total story, or situation. The story may be presented in a series of pictures, or film shots, with the sentences given in the sound channel for repetition by the student. The story is repeated two or three times, each time removing more information from the sound channel, which the learner will have had to remember. In the end, the learner will be producing a short, spoken, controlled composition. It is one step further on from single examples of spoken structure; here the sequence of sentences will have a meaning and an interest beyond the structural framework. Further stories might be presented in visual form, with superimposed printed 'key-words' to assist the learner to say the right kind of sentence.

A short dramatized sequence might show the following story: a shop-owner is woken up by the police who take him to his shop.

We see the window broken, and the safe open, and we are told that a lot of money has been stolen. The owner is given some tea and taken home. We see the police arrest the thief on the following day. This story can then be retold in stills, or film with frames frozen at certain points. The verb forms are superimposed on the pictures: *was woken up/was taken/had been broken/had been opened/had been stolen/was given/was taken home/was caught.* The viewer-learner has to tell the story, using the given verb forms. He will have to produce the rest of the sentences from his own memory and understanding of the original story-presentation, and within his own range of spoken language facility. At a later stage, such a procedure might dispense with the key-words altogether, simply asking the viewer to retell the story in his own words. There can be no check upon correct response with a home viewer, but the class could handle such a technique under the teacher's supervision. Instead of using key-words, a story might be accompanied by questions in the sound channel; the answers, when given in sequence, then form the spoken composition. Such techniques allow for a gradual decrease in the control which is exercised over the student's production by varying the amount of given material.

Guided written composition techniques, in addition to controlling structure choice, also attempt at a later stage to control semantic choice within a story framework. A television treatment might be as follows: the viewer is asked to select one of two pictures; say a teacher or a postman. A story is then told which involves choices at certain points. These choices depend upon the viewer's first choice of character. Double pictures would be shown, or split-screen film, at each stage of the story's development. 'He's going to the bookcase/letter-box; he's picking up the books/letters; he's putting them in his case/bag; he's walking to the school/post-office; he's talking to some other teachers/postmen'; and so on. Additional help (or control) may be provided by clues in the sound channel, or in superimposed word captions. At each stage, the viewer-learner is asked to say the correct sentence out loud. Such a procedure requires two or three repetitions until the viewer is following the sequence of pictures, and making the correct semantic decisions, with some fluency.

A varied range of visual material is available to provide stimuli for creative speech on the part of the viewers. Viewers may be asked to describe events in a film, with or without specified constraints upon the manner of expression they use. A man may be filmed driving a car, and viewers asked to use the present continuous tense: 'He's turning left . . . he's stopping . . . he's crossing the road . . . he's switching on the radio.' An experiment may be described aloud: 'The water was poured into the beaker . . . the beaker and the water were weighed . . . the beaker was heated . . .'. Aerial photographs, timetables for railways or aeroplanes, graphs, plans of houses—all these and more might be employed as a basis for spoken compositions of varying kinds. Viewers can be asked how to get from one place to another, how long certain journeys take, which type of transport would be quicker and cheaper for certain journeys, whether there are any mistakes in an architect's plans, and so on. In each case, structural control can be exerted to a greater or lesser extent; examples may be needed before the viewer can be asked to produce any language himself.

Learners also need to be able to respond to situational stimuli as well as verbal or graphic stimuli. Different styles may be required for different types of people, certain conversational formulae are useful and may be inserted into an English course. They have already been mentioned in connection with practice in intonation patterns. This practice may now be incorporated into situational dialogues which illustrate features of spoken style, both in intonational features and in choice of words employed. Short interchanges to ask a stranger the time, or a direction; to ask the people next door to turn their radio down —people that you know and people that you have never met before; dialogues asking for information, for advice, asking for something to be done: all these may be demonstrated clearly and rapidly on television, and then the viewer may be asked to take first one part and then another. It is in this area that a great deal of our normal everyday conversation takes place; and it is in this area that practice is most difficult to arrange in a teaching situation. The teacher, in the classroom or on television, can only show the type of language that might be used in certain situations, between certain types of people. Systematically to present the multitudinous variations on this theme would be out of the question. Practice is therefore impossible to achieve outside the environment in which the language is used as mother-tongue. All we can do is present a variety of speech situations for recognition, and use them in a small way as practice material for the learner-speaker.

Notes

1. Ray Bradbury: *Fahrenheit 451* Hart-Davis 1954
2. Lina Graham: 'Pupil Participation in the Teaching of Languages by Television' *E.T.I.* Vol. 1 No. 4 Dec. 1967
3. Pierre Léon: 'Teaching Pronunciation' in Valdman (ed.) op. cit. 1966 p. 71
4. John Laver: 'The Production of Speech' in *New Horizons in Linguistics* (ed. John Lyons) Penguin 1970
5. S. Pit Corder: 'Language Teaching by Television' in Valdman (ed.) 1966, pp. 242–3
6. David Abercrombie: 'Conversation and Spoken Prose'. Reprinted in *Studies in Phonetics and Linguistics* Oxford University Press 1965
7. S. C. Murison-Bowie: *Contact 1: The Oxford Secondary English Course, Ethiopia* Oxford University Press 1970

7 Television and the Reading Skill

Having dealt with the skills of oracy, we turn to the literate skills. Large areas of the world continue to yield statistics showing high illiteracy rates, and schemes for dealing with the problem are many and various. Efforts in this field have brought about a considerable academic emphasis upon the problems of reading, and this concern seems in no way to be abating. The existence of a 'new electric technology that threatens this ancient technology of literacy'[1] has not driven governments of largely illiterate areas to bypass their literacy projects. The book as an individual information-retrieval system is unlikely to be replaced by computerized home libraries of tapes and microfilm. The reverse side of the printed instructions which enable us to understand and operate a TV set, is the TV programme which can help us to read the printed instructions.

The Physical Aspects of Reading

The demands of world literacy, and the accompanying academic interest in the reading skill, have produced a wide variety of theories and methods to assist teachers and learners. Many of these relate directly to the way the printed material is presented, and the printed information which should be given emphasis. The alphabetic, syllabic or phonic methods emphasize the graphic information presented in units smaller than the word; the word and sentence methods place greater importance upon reading large units of printed information. The larger the unit selected, the more importance is placed upon 'meaningful' reading. The smaller the unit, the greater the importance placed upon the relationship between reading and other language skills—speech, and the identification of phonic relationships, and writing, and the identification of letter shapes. Both areas require attention, as an analysis of poor readers indicates. Readers need to be able to both synthesize graphic symbols into words and structures, and to analyse them in order to perceive such problems as *bid/did* or *man/mane*.[2] Methods of presenting the material to be read depend upon the interpretation placed upon the known facts about how we perceive graphic symbols. Eye-movements have been studied among readers of different cultural and educational backgrounds, and have been observed to have the same features. The eyes move along a line of written material in an irregular fashion, called saccadic movements; our eyes pause at certain points, called fixations; what we perceive clearly at each fixation is called the eye-span. Unlike the listening skill, the reading skill enables us to go back over material, and in practice our eyes continually regress over longer and shorter lengths of writing. Studies of good readers show that they tend to have more regular eye-movements, shorter fixations, wider eye-span and fewer regressions. This fact has encouraged a number of courses in reading techniques to aim at developing these physical skills of reading perception, by means of mechanical devices such as tachistoscopes and pacers. The features of these machines have been embodied into a number of filmed courses for the teaching of reading, and could therefore be adapted to television with relative ease. Before leaping into such practices with a television course, however, it has to be recognized that eye-training is only part of the business of reading. It can be argued that our eye-movements during reading are so rapid that we stand no more chance of controlling them than we do of controlling the eardrum in its vibrating reaction to sound. It has also been argued that the movements of the eye will develop in their own way if the material presented to them for reading is well-graded, interesting and clearly laid out. Finally, the observable facts of eye-movements during reading do not explain why the eye moves as it does. The success which is reported with courses which specialize in training eye-movements cannot take into account a wide variety of other factors which undoubtedly influence our ability to read. Our concentration varies constantly as we read. Our memory of what we read may last for no more than a few sentences. Different types of written material involve different types of reading skill, and we may apply the wrong technique, skimming where we should read slowly and carefully. Most important of all, our understanding of what we read may be faulty, and this affects our reading efficiency far more drastically than our eye-span, length of fixation and number of regressions. These physical features are important, but they probably reflect our comprehension of the material, rather than the reverse.

Faulty comprehension may be linguistic in origin, and will depend upon our grasp of other language skills as well as our ability to read. We may not recognize a written word or sentence; we may not be able to say it out loud; even then, we may not understand the spoken form. Speech and the understanding of speech is an important element in reading. When children first begin to read, they read aloud. As their reading efficiency improves they read silently, though it seems likely that 'inner speech' continues. Learners of a second language may bypass the vocalization stage of reading in the second language, depending upon the stage they have reached in their first language. But they will probably need to continue mentally to say the words they read and do not understand from their written form alone. Graphic symbols inadequately convey the range of spoken language, especially those features of meaning conveyed by intonation and stress. An inability to relate written sentences to their spoken form will hinder comprehension as will the failure to recognize the spoken form when it is produced from the graphic representation. Lastly faulty comprehension of written material may be non-linguistic—may be a failure to understand the cultural ambiance of the passage, the style of writing, the conventions of written communication which native-speakers have come to recognize, as in advertisements, directions, signwriting and so on.

The teaching of reading therefore demands an eclectic approach, since each individual will have different problems, some perceptual, some related to general intelligence and comprehension, some related to concentration and memory. In general, it seems that the more a person reads, the better he becomes at it. A television course in reading, therefore, has an immediate problem:

it cannot possibly provide the quantity of written material which a learner will require. A second problem is that individual differences are very significant in reading, as in writing, while television aims at the mass, and has to make arbitrary decisions as to the pacing of material, perceptual problems, and the quantity of material relative to concentration and memory span. How television approaches the teaching of reading in a particular system will depend upon measures taken elsewhere in the system to deal with the problem. It may be of use in the pre-reading stage of perceptual training, in presenting different types of material to explain reading-speed techniques, in rapidly demonstrating similar letter forms, or phonic relationships. In none of these areas can television present the amount of practice material required, nor can it cope with individual differences among the viewer-learners. It may, however, be able to suggest new methods to the classroom teacher, or to concentrate upon one technique while the teacher deals with others. As we go through the three levels of difficulty in the reading skill, it must be remembered that we are simply making an inventory of possible uses of television in the teaching of reading. From this inventory, the course constructor can select those areas where he feels television can help most in his particular synthesis, applicable to his particular teaching system.

Phonics

Fry, in his book on techniques for reading faster, suggests the necessity of separating 'oral reading skills from silent reading skills', since the habit of vocalizing the words we read tends to slow us down and impair our efficient reading ability.[3] Macmillan, however, points out that this is probably not possible, and even if it were, it may not be desirable.[4] He cites those features of intonation and stress, often essential to meaning, which are not adequately conveyed by graphic symbols, and which a native-speaker automatically recognizes in written material, possibly because he is able to 'vocalize' the written symbols in his head. This is not the same as saying that 'speech is primary', and that a language-learner should not read anything he has not already heard and spoken, as some methods advocate. In the majority of cases, it is not necessary to vocalize, or sub-vocalize, written material in order to understand it. It is not extraordinary that words such as *hippopotamus*, or *kangaroo* should occur in readers for children who are just learning to read; nor is it necessary that they should be able to say these words before they read them. Such words have a distinctive, recognizable shape which children can understand and easily memorize. Such shapes are easier to read, perhaps, than pairs of words such as *horse/house*, or *door/ deer*. There seems little doubt that an ability to associate spellings with sounds is very useful for children learning to read. If, later, they are able to bypass this stage in the large number of cases of words they meet, the ability will still be a useful tool when they meet new words which give them difficulty. Hill and Ure mention the word *breat* which would give difficulty to a native-speaker because he would not know whether to associate it with *great*, *beat* or *threat*.[5] The development of such associations is an essential part of reading technique, and the foreign-language learner needs practice in this technique to enable him to make generalizations about the words he meets, and relate them to new words. The teacher needs to identify areas of possible difficulty where recourse to pronunciation will assist recognition. Practice in these areas then needs to be provided.

Some television series have already included such practice in phonics, by incorporating 'morphophone spots', which draw the viewer-learner's attention to a spelling-sound relationship.[6] In a spoken story, several words are incorporated which contain the same sound. As each of these words is spoken, the written form is presented on the screen. The sound symbol being practised appears immediately under the same symbol as it appears in the previous word. At the end, the viewer has a graph in which the particular symbol appears in a straight column. This procedure can be graded, so that the sound-symbol is shown, first in an initial position, then medial, then final, and then in any position in a word. The story may be illustrated by film or by pictures, and the words superimposed upon the picture to one side of the screen, written on a separate caption and revealed one by one. In the early stages of this type of practice, a symbol-to-sound, one-to-one relationship will be dealt with. Subsequently, practice should be given in those symbols which are often used for more than one sound: for example, *g—gun, girl, big/gentleman, general, gipsy.* This is probably most useful with vowel sounds which often cause difficulty: *piece, feet, leaf,* and *caught, bought, fort, ball, board, lawn,* and so on. Short anecdotes, told in words and pictures, can be used to demonstrate these relationships, and practice can be given by the presentation of further material on the same lines. Other features which can be handled in this way are such items as suffixes, prefixes, inflectional endings, silent *e,* unexploded plosives at the ends of words, and so forth. Having contextualized such features in a story, they can then be recapitulated by simple presentation of the words, individually or in graph form, with the relevant symbol underlined, while the word is repeated in the sound channel. Having completed sufficient practice of this nature, the material may be tested by the presentation of multiple spellings in the visual channel, together with a single pronunciation in the sound channel. The multiple spellings might then dissolve to the correct spelling plus a confirming picture, with a repetition of the correct pronunciation. Thus, the word *selling* might be heard, together with the four spellings *sailing/selling/ceiling/sealing* shown on the screen. Three unrelated spellings would then disappear, leaving the correct spelling with an accompanying picture showing a shop salesman in action. The word *selling* would then be repeated in the sound channel. At a later stage, the learner might be asked to say the sound emphasized in a list of printed words, such as *bit/orange/women/minute;* he may be asked to say whether the sounds are the same or different. Another exercise might present four pictures, each demonstrating a printed word superimposed upon them, such as *meal/seat/great/leaf.* The learner is then asked to select in which word the emphasized sound is different from the others. By means of animated captions, or animated film, the particular sound we are interested in (here printed in heavy type) can be isolated on television; words can be made to split apart to demonstrate phonic relationships, and then to coalesce to show how sounds and symbols join together to make spoken and written words. Such a technique can demonstrate how sounds vary in value according to context: *d* in *doing, find, grandfather; p* in *putting, trap, raspberry.* Similarly, demonstrations of different spellings related to the same sound can be shown. Letters can be made to appear from nowhere on the screen, to disappear, to move about on the screen, to rearrange themselves into different spellings, and so on. As with exercise material in the other skills, the advantage on television here is the ability to present a large number of exercises simply and rapidly. The instructions to the viewer have to be clear in each case, and several examples of the same type of exercise should be given at any one time, rather than moving at random from one type of exercise to another.

Pre-reading Training

In some languages, the sound-symbol relationship is different to that of English. Certain languages, for example, relate a written symbol to a whole syllable. Extra phonic practice may be necessary for users of such systems, especially in such features of English as consonant clusters. Similarly, users of such writing systems may require extra practice before we come to teach them the recognition of the English symbols themselves. Such pre-reading training is especially useful with young learners. Left-to-right eye-movements may be encouraged by means of demonstrating such movements in the studio, on film, or with animated captions. The viewer has to follow a ball as it moves from left to right across the screen, or a pattern which appears from left to right on the screen. A train might take one of three or four tracks, all moving from left to right to different destinations; the viewer has to follow the tracks with his eyes, to find out which one the train will go to. The train can then be animated across the screen. Pictures might be built up in sections, which appear in a left-to-right sequence across the screen. For example, a fish might be built up in four sections, a snake in five sections. When spellings are introduced, each section of the picture can be shown with a letter, so that the picture and the word are built up from left to right for the viewer. Later still, sentences might be built up in the same way, to demonstrate left-to-right layout. Sometimes, early readers experience difficulty in following written symbols from the end of one line to the beginning of the next. Practice can be simply given in this skill by building up pictures in rows from left to right across the screen, before moving on to similar practice with words.

Exercises of this nature do not require prolonged, intensive practice; rather, they should be occasionally introduced into a programme, integrated so that the eye-movement practice is incidental to other practice contained in the visual material being presented.

Other pre-reading practice is sometimes given to learners in the form of shape-recognition. Whether this is included in a systematic approach to teaching reading depends upon the skill of the learner in reading his own native language. It is something which television can handle, probably more easily than the teacher in the classroom. A viewer might be asked to find two similar shapes among a group of half a dozen. The shapes might all be upright to begin with, and then at different angles. A picture might be shown with one piece missing. The bottom half of the TV screen can present three or four alternative shapes, and the viewer has to select visually the shape which will fit into the missing part of the picture. Such exercises can be graded in complexity; the aim is gradually to introduce letter shapes for the viewer to recognize and differentiate. This type of practice becomes most useful when viewers are selecting between letters of similar shape, such as *d/b/ p/q*, *m/n*, *c/e/o* and so on. In addition to letter shapes, it may be useful to present word shapes in blocks of similar outline, such as *fish/book/desk*, or *big/hop/tap*. Again, such shapes can be made to appear and disappear, and to move about the screen to demonstrate similarities.

Recognition of the Graphic Symbols

When we come to the teaching of reading itself, our approach will depend upon the overall method selected for the particular education system. As we have said, both analytic and synthetic skills are required; every reader constantly builds up and breaks down the material he reads, in different places, in different moods, in different environmental conditions. Concentration, memory, reading experience, general intelligence—all these contribute to the effectiveness of our reading at any one time. A method for teaching reading has to deal with recognition of larger units and of smaller units—with the wood and the trees. Different methods simply lay down different priorities—the letter, the syllable, the word, the sentence—according to the learner's native writing system, or the course writer's predilection for a particular theory and classroom method. Television might be employed for any of these methods, and an inventory of its uses should deal with them all.

From the pre-reading stage of shape identification, it is a natural development to the stage of letter identification. There are various opinions as to the order in which the letters should be introduced, and whether upper or lower case should be presented first. Fries grades capital letters into those made up of lines, those made up of curves, and those made up of both. Any system will serve, so long as it is consistent. Here, there are often differences between printed and written letter forms—as in the letters 'a/f/g/ l'—and the learner may have to be taught both forms, according to the method of presentation. In a television programme, the letters may be printed on captions; they may be shown being written. Television is ideally suited to the presentation of the reading system, which contextualizes a letter by showing a picture of an object, the initial letter of which is incorporated into the picture—an *s* shape depicted as a snake, for example. This system raises the whole question of meaning in the teaching of reading in early stages. Letters are as useless as abstract shapes if they are not given some special meaning for the learner—if the learner cannot perceive where this basic practice will ultimately lead him. It may be useful, therefore, to identify these shapes by giving them their names. Exercises in letter recognition cannot get very far without the learner's ability to identify letters by name. Naming letters, however, carries its own problems when children relate the names to the sounds the letters produce when spoken in words. If exercises in phonics are being incorporated into the reading system, the learner has to be given a systematic formula to help him: 'This letter is called "a", and in this word its sound is . . .'. Exercises in letter recognition in a television programme can take several forms, and can be made visually exciting and stimulating by means of animated film or captions, or by using cut-out letters in a studio with puppets or presenters. One programme in an American series shows the letter *w*, which is gradually eaten away by a puppet forming the letters *n*, *v* and *i* as it does so. A jumbled group of letters might be shown, and the viewer asked to pick out all the *s* shapes he can find. Pictures of objects or actions might be shown, together with a letter, and the viewer asked to say whether it is the correct initial letter of the object's name. Attention can be drawn to difficult spelling features, by showing pictures with printed words in which the relevant letters are missing: *sle—e/bri—e/ba—e/ju—e*—omitting *dg* in each case. At the letter stage, it may be useful to speed up letter recognition by using a flashcard technique which systematically reduces the amount of time the students have to perceive and recognize a letter. Television can electronically duplicate the mechanism of the tachistoscope, which is frequently used in classrooms for this purpose. A caption camera can be controlled by a switching device which regulates the time of each exposure, and the gap between each exposure. Its main use is in teaching students to perceive whole words and groups of words, and we shall discuss its uses again a little later. But it might be a useful device for revising letter-recognition and letter-naming functions.

Probably the majority of recent reading courses have been based upon the 'whole-word' method, preferring to encourage learner-readers to recognize the shape of a total word, and later deal with specific problems of letter differentiation. The vagaries of English orthography defy a completely phonic approach to word recognition. Techniques have to emphasize a consistent recognition of word shape, though a symbol-sound connection can often be of use to trigger the learner's memory. To begin, written words need to be related to the objects they represent. Real objects in a studio may have name-cards attached to them, and simple situations (in a shop or street setting) can provide a context for this kind of naming activity. Alternatively, written names might be superimposed upon drawing or photographs, the written form of verbs might be superimposed upon a film in which the action is frozen for a few seconds. The selection and grading of words for this kind of activity may be based upon a number of criteria—contextual, word-counts, and so on. At some time in the course, it may be necessary to emphasize words which, because of their form, cause particular problems of recognition. Certain words—*place/palace, very/every*—are confused because the reader makes omissions in his perception of them. Other words are sometimes read in reverse—*saw/was, no/on*. Sometimes the similar form of words leads to complete substitutions—*swim/swan, these/those, car/can*, and so on. Learners can also be encouraged to recognize recurring features in words by grouping them together in the presentation stage. Prefixes, suffixes, inflectional endings, and such special features as the 'silent' *e* in words can be given special presentation to give the learner further recognition clues. Again, animated film or captions can be used to visually emphasize these features, common to a group of words shown on the screen. Initial practice of word recognition then concentrates on word-picture relationships, requiring the learner to choose from a selection the correct word for a particular picture, or the correct picture for a given word. More elaborate exercises in visual discrimination between words of similar design might be given later; the word *house* might be shown in the top half of the screen, and the words *horse/whose/house/hours* in the bottom half. The student has to find the matching word. In giving the correct answer, the word should be supplemented with a picture of the named object, to confirm meaning and reinforce the learner's correct identification of the word shape. Home viewers may wish to point to the correct word in such a group. Children in a classroom will not be able to demonstrate to their teacher that they have in fact selected the correct word, and it may be necessary to number the choices, and to ask the children to call out the number of the correct answer. In one television reading scheme for children learning at home, the home learner was provided with word cards related to the content of the programmes. A particular word was then shown in the top half of the screen; the child at home selected the card containing the correct word and held it up to the bottom half of the screen. A similar technique could be used with children in classrooms, each given a variety of cards related to the content of the particular day's TV lesson. They could be asked to hold up the card which matches the word being shown on the screen, and the teacher in the classroom could then check the response.

The Perception of Word Groups

At the level of the word and the group of words, recognition train-ing can be assisted by the use of a tachistoscope, whose function can be simulated in a television camera. Developed initially for rapid identification of aircraft, the system in no way simulates what actually happens when we read. The timed exposure of a word or group of words can only help to develop our ability to perceive the exposed material more rapidly, though this may simply be a training in concentration. During the gaps between exposure, the student learns to concentrate harder in preparation for taking in the next exposure. After considerable practice, less concentration is required. When he actually reads lines of print, however, the concentration factor is normally less important at the level of per-ception than at the level of structural and semantic complexity. Unlike language he hears, the language he reads is available for regression, rereadings, and even rapid skimming if it is of little interest to him. The timed exposure of word groups compels equal concentration every time. Further, it assumes that all learners will 'fix' their eyes at roughly the same points in a line of print. Even in those filmed courses which allow some latitude in points of fixa-tion, there is not that freedom to regress which is a feature of even the most efficient reading. However short the exposure-time, learners will tend to make two or three fixations, backwards and forwards, in order to perceive the total grouping. Whether it is a picture of an aeroplane, or the picture of a word, it is likely that perception is the result of several impressions of details which together lead to the total picture, and that this is what is meant by perceiving the picture 'as a whole'. What constitutes the 'point of fixation' and what constitutes 'peripheral vision' is then a way of categorizing the features requiring more or less concentration in building the total perception. In recognizing an aeroplane, the perceiver's points of fixation will be conditioned by what he has been taught to look out for; the more complex these details are, the longer the fixations will tend to be. Similarly, in perceiving words and groups of words, the learner needs to be taught what to look out for. Perception is conditioned by his knowledge of the language, his familiarity with the way it is structured, and the complexity of the meaning conveyed. To train his perception of word groups, without reference to the structural and semantic levels of language, is therefore a pointless exercise. It would be like training a student to rapidly recognize lists of telephone numbers, without telling him whose telephone numbers they were.

Once the student has mastered particular structural features of the language, and knows their meaning when he reads them, it is a useful exercise to speed up his reading of them by the use of tachistoscope procedures. It should not be necessary for a reader to linger over each word in verb phrases—'They are walking', 'He is speaking'—or in prepositional phrases—'in the box', 'on the table'. In such groupings, certain features are common, and should be recognized more easily than other features. Thus, it is likely that the reader will concentrate upon *they* and *walk*, and that *are* and *-ing* will require less concentration. Similarly, the preposition and article will probably require less concentration than the noun in the prepositional phrase, though prepositions of similar shape—*in*, *on*—may cause perceptual problems. By grouping words according to structure in this way, the use of timed exposures helps to increase the learner's familiarity with the common features of the structure, and to speed up his recognition of them. The rapid presentation of many structures of the same type will encourage the learner to concentrate on the new item in each group, and allow his 'peripheral vision' to take care of the familiar part of each group. From the verb phrase and the prepositional phrase, the grading might extend to simple noun phrases, short relative clauses and so on. At a later stage, short connected prose, specially written, might be presented in a series of timed exposures. It must be emphasized, however, that this procedure bears little relationship to the actual performance of the learner who reads lines of print. Where this system has been adopted in a television course in faster reading, attempts were made to time the exposures accurately, and to time the gaps between each exposure. By accurate timing, the aim is to gradually shorten the time of each exposure, and to compel the reader to concentrate, or 'fix', on the crucial element in the word-group. The danger here is that, in transmitting such material to a mass audience, it is not possible to gauge the rate of speed-up with any accuracy. A control group might be used, where it is possible to collect a group representative of the viewing audience. The progress of the control group can then be measured and the television course graded accordingly. It will also be possible to gauge from the control group the amount of time to leave between each exposure. In early lessons, it will be necessary to leave more time for the students to digest each exposure before proceeding to the next; this gap may subsequently be shortened. The viewers' attention needs to be drawn to the area of the screen where the exposed word group will appear, perhaps by retaining an outline of the slot in which the words will be shown. In some filmed courses, a central dot is shown between each exposure, in the hope that the student will perceive the next word group from the centre of the slot outwards. In practice, however, this procedure may be a hindrance; the key-word in the group, requiring most concentration, may well be at the end of the slot. These problems will vary from country to country, and with different age-groups, and it may be necessary to run pre-tests with the help of specially written slides for tachistoscope, in order to ascertain the best method to adopt, and the best exposure-speed at which to begin the course.

Varieties of Graphic Style

Before leaving the perceptual problems of the reading skill, and proceeding to the level of structure, there are a few more points which need to be made. The physical situation of the viewer-learner is of particular importance when we put words on the screen. In general we may say that the course for home-viewers can afford to have many more words on the screen at any one time, than the course for students in a classroom. Questions of layout, type-face, and so on are of relevance here, and, in so far as is possible, experiments should be run in a typical viewing situation to establish the best possible presentation of written material on the screen, from the point of view of quantity, spacing and contrast. For more advanced students, it may be useful to incorporate special practice in the recognition of different type-faces. Stylized lettering, such as is used in advertisements, shop-signs, packaged goods, and so on, can all be integrated into a television programme, to give incidental practice in recognizing them. Similarly, attempts should be made to incorporate handwriting into a television programme, for the purpose of recognition practice. Whatever system of handwriting is adopted in the English teaching course, or whatever attitude is adopted towards the teaching of handwriting, there is no doubt that students will have to learn to read other people's writing styles. A television presentation can not only demonstrate various handwriting styles; it can also show a hand actually forming the words in a particular style; and it can split the screen so as to show the same words in print and in handwriting. This particular skill is hardly ever dealt with in a native-language, and it leads to long periods of laborious familiarization with different writing styles. This is much more difficult for a second-language learner whose native writing style is totally different. Regular practice in handwriting recognition through the means of television can alleviate what might prove an intractable problem if not dealt with elsewhere in the teaching system.

The Recognition of Written Structures

The structural level of the reading skill has frequently been neglected by course writers, since reading has usually been considered a secondary activity to speech. If the learner can say what he reads, he can understand what he reads—so runs the theory. Yet in the very first year of English instruction, the classroom teacher has to make some decisions about what he will tell his class about spoken and written English. Certain structures are normally taught, in spoken language, as contractions—*he's, they're, doesn't, aren't.* When the teacher turns to the teaching of structural reading, he has to decide whether to teach these forms, or the full forms normally found in written language. As the English course proceeds, these decisions cannot be deferred for long. When we read a page of English, we perform dozens of grammatical operations, some of which we may never use in speech.[7] The whole area of writing 'style' is largely a question of structural arrangement. This is a far more carefully considered production of structure than is possible when we create speech.

A structure such as the non-defining relative clause ('My father whose business frequently took him abroad, knew Spain well') is a feature of written English rather than spoken English. Many other structures come within the same category: 'David, a fisherman by profession, . . . '; 'Having discussed the matter for some time, we . . . '; 'Rarely had he seen such beauty . . .'. Such examples occur in the advanced stages of an English course. Nonetheless, they indicate that a course in structural reading cannot simply be an extension of a course in spoken English. Filmed ELT courses frequently present dramatic situations, and emphasize the structures used by intermittent sections in which the structures are written down. These are presumably intended to reinforce the learner's ability to understand the spoken dialogue. Yet a word-count of early readers for children would probably place such words as *you, we, I*, and the present continuous tense (common in spoken English), well below the third person forms, singular and plural, and the present simple and the past tenses. Written dialogue, with its approximations to speech, has to be read, naturally, but a structurally graded reading course would not make it a priority. The 'literary' aspect of reading material needs to be emphasized from the beginning.

In presenting items in a structural reading course, there should be no difficulty in the material from the point of view of lexical meaning. As we shall see, comprehension at this stage needs to be concentrated upon the structure under consideration, and not with the meaning which the structure embodies. We are teaching the students to recognize the structural systems of written English, and to increase their familiarity with them; this aim is frustrated if they also are confused by the underlying meaning. Television can be of assistance here. The early readers given to children are liberally sprinkled with illustrations. The illustrations present the underlying meaning of the written material, putting it in perspective. Television can continue this practice throughout the reading course. The danger is that the learner guesses at the meaning of the material, or guesses at the structure being employed, from perusal of the illustrations. Care must be taken to ensure that the accompanying pictures do not take the place of the text and that the learner's need to understand the words— his motivation—is not short-circuited by the pictures. For example, a picture of a brush, and the written word 'brush', might be presented simultaneously. It is then pointless to ask the viewer what the word says, since the answer is provided visually.

A reading course might decide to begin with the form of the present simple tense. A picture of a girl is shown; a voice says: 'This is Jenny. What does she do everyday? Read this story.' The title, 'Everyday', is then shown, and explained. Then a sequence of words is written on the screen, and the relevant structural item—third person singular final *s*—is isolated by means of animation. We might decide to use a sequence such as *gets up/eats/walks/sits/plays*. Later we might go on to *washes/brushes/fetches/races*. A picture of each activity is shown *after* the written structure has been shown; this confirms understanding, and does not hinder the learner's need to read the words. After presentation in this way, a testing sequence might use the same material, but showing the picture together with the written structure. The student has then to say whether the structure he reads corresponds with the picture he sees. A similar set of still pictures could be used for the past tense, beginning the series with the title 'Yesterday'. A diary might be shown on the screen as a framework for the reading practice, cutting away to pictures or film to confirm what the student has read. Imperative forms, common in printed instructions, might be set in the context of a recipe, or building a model, or looking for buried treasure. Again, the written structure should be presented before the visual which confirms the meaning. When a picture-structure sequence is complete, the structures themselves can be presented on the screen, laid out so as to emphasize the crucial elements, underneath each other, or mixed into each other. This points the structural generalization which the student should be making from the examples. Where the generalization involves transformations of some kind, the use of word-animation can often point the operation being employed. In a series on reported speech, we might show the speaker in a lecture and a student reporting what he says. The speaker might be shown saying the words; we then freeze the film and superimpose a balloon caption with the words written down. We then mix to the student's notebook where the reported form of the words appears through the actual words spoken. Instead of film, we might use still photographs with balloon captions.

The old silent-film technique can also be of use in presenting written material. A filmed story might be shown, with crucial plot elements every so often; these can be filled by written captions, designed to use the structure under scrutiny. This system might be used for such structures as time clauses ('While he was waiting, his friend phoned the police'), or participial constructions ('Having found the house, they knocked on the door'). The use of subtitles can also be useful for certain types of story, where the accompanying visual does not distract from the need to read the words. Three people might be shown in a lift which has got stuck. The film might show each character in turn, and subtitle: 'David, who was a teacher, knocked on the door'; 'Tom, who was a builder, knocked on the roof'; and so on. The story might proceed, using a variation of the structure, and subtitling: 'Tom, whose hobby was mountain-climbing, tried to climb the rope'; 'Fred, whose foot was in plaster, sat on the floor'; and so on.

The written material should be set into a literary context wherever possible—retelling a story, reading instructions, writing a report. After each demonstration segment, the structures should be brought together on the screen, to demonstrate their similar elements. It may be necessary to put them on a roller caption, so that they roll from the bottom of the screen to the top.[8] Care should be taken over the number of words on the screen at any one time, and over the speed with which they rolled. Special practice may be given, with well-known structures, in speed reading, duplicating the function of the mechanical reading pacer which is sometimes used for individual reading tuition. Having pre-tested a representative section of the viewing audience, the structures might be rolled across the screen at an average pace, forcing the viewer to take in the words before they disappear. One of the most important elements in efficient reading is the reader's ability to recognize structures, rather than single words. The television tachistoscope technique is useful here. Complex structures can be split up into sections, and each section exposed in turn for a fixed time. 'My brother Tom,/who works in London,/keeps rabbits'; 'Having mended the puncture,/he drove away'; 'He didn't know/whether they lived there'. This kind of exercise should not be covered in the same lesson as the structure is presented; it should be reserved for a later stage in recognition practice.

Viewer Response

A television reading course has to make provision for student response, to test whether the structures being taught have been understood, and will be consistently recognized. In writing comprehension material at this level, the aim is simply to test structure comprehension, rather than to check understanding of the underlying meaning. The most efficient method of achieving this is to provide question sheets in ancillary material sent out to viewing students. Reading material containing the questions can then be presented on the screen, and the viewer-learner can be asked to check his answers on the sheets sent to him. Questions might be in the form of fill-in-the-blank exercises, or the selection of the correct answer from a list of possible answers. These formats might be provided in ancillary material sent to the student, or they may be shown on the screen, with enough time allowed for the viewers to respond. Where transformations are required, one film series has designed an elaborate range of symbols as cueing devices for viewers; these are used to denote present tense structures which should be changed to the past form or the future form, to denote the formation of a question, and a variety of other desired responses. Response is most often in the form of reading aloud, incorporating the missing word, especially where answer sheets are provided, or calling out the number of the right answer, or ticking the correct answer on an answer sheet. The method chosen will depend upon the type and physical situation of the viewing audience, and whether there is a supervising teacher or not. Responding to questions on written material presented on television has one great disadvantage. Whereas a student can refer back to written passages in textbooks to find answers to questions, the television screen cannot retain enough written information for the viewer to do the same. Memory is therefore a crucial factor. One way of avoiding this problem is to ask the question before the written material is presented for reading. Even when the questions are reserved until the end of the reading passage, the answer format—blank-filling or multiple-choice—should be designed to provide enough clues to remind the viewer of the reading passage and enable him to answer. It is his recognition of the structure which is being tested here, not his memory of informational details in the passage.

Reading for Understanding

One would suppose that the only motivation which would prompt a learner to persevere with reading practice would be the hope of understanding the meaning encased in the words. In his book on reading, Fries seems to think that, in the early stages of reading, the meaning of the words is not very important. He maintains that 'extraneous interest in a story as a story' is likely to hinder the child in his struggle to unravel the words and structures.[9] From the success of a number of exceedingly dull children's books, he may well be right that the child's success in mastering the symbols themselves is sufficient motivation. The problem is somewhat different, however, in the case of the second-language learner who is linguistically proficient in his first language. His motivation will suffer if he struggles through his symbol-recognition procedures, to find he has mastered, 'A cat bats at a rat.' For the secondary school student and for the adult, there is a paucity of reading material aimed at absolute beginners. There is a good deal of research behind the functional literacy campaigns which have sprung up in underdeveloped parts of the world, and some of this research could well be directed towards the problem of the older second-language learner. In these areas, the first readers are aimed at such problems as malaria eradication, basic hygiene, basic agriculture. Books taught to the women of Uganda explain their legal rights to them in simple language. For the older learner, such interest is an integral part of learning to read. Depending upon the type of audience, the reading course, in textbook or on television, cannot avoid for very long the third level of language difficulty—the level of meaning.

The second-language learner is likely to meet many types of different written material, and he needs experience of a number of them. Some of these materials he will need for reference purposes, some for information, some he will need to interpret according to his own requirements, and some he will want to read simply for enjoyment. Most early readers simply provide stories, factual or fictional, and this reflects the traditional view of language learning as a means of reading literature. This is undoubtedly an important aspect of the reading skill, but may not be what is required for a particular audience. Informational material is of equal importance, as is contained in newspapers, travel brochures, highway codes, booklets of health precautions, cookery books, and so on. People need to understand street signs, directions for finding something or somewhere, instructions on using medicine, packet foods, telephone directories. The type of material employed will depend upon the status of English in the country (a second or foreign language), the likely demands of the students, the age and environment, and other factors. A secondary school system which uses English as the medium of instruction will want their English classes to use reading material from other subject areas. Learners may want to use reference books, such as dictionaries, or encyclopaedias, and may require instruction in the use of a library, and how to find information from the contents section, or the index of a book. In addition to the type of written material, there are a variety of styles, some of which students should become acquainted with. Certain writing is formal, some informal; some is in the form of detailed, logical argument; some writing is personal while some is objective. We have already seen that the graphic symbols of English do not adequately convey the full range of meaning, and that the native speaker-reader will impose intonation and stress features, subconsciously, upon the material he reads; it will be impossible to train the second-language learner systematically in all these refinements, but he should at least be made aware, at some stage, of the variety of style and multiplicity of interpretations which written English can convey.

A television reading course cannot provide the quantity of written material which is necessary to train a learner to read. It can, however, satisfactorily demonstrate the variety of written English, provide introductory material, and allow the teacher with the ancillary material to produce follow-up material in quantity. With the help of pictures, studio situations, and film, television can present the extra-linguistic context of each type of written material: the sick villager, in need of elementary instruction in health precautions; the policeman writing his report; the journalist reporting on an interview he has had; library scenes; street scenes when we are looking at shop signs, and so on. The style of each type of writing can be shown: typewriting, print, handwriting, signwriting. A whole range of typographical material can be brought into use: graphs, aeroplane timetables, charts, maps, catalogues, posters, lists, advertisements in newspapers, packages of various kinds. Each can be integrated into a television programme, and used to give practice in reading. Some of this material can be presented on the screen in its original form; some will have to be rewritten, and set out in a more accessible form. A caption-roller may be used, or slides, or the camera might tilt down the lines of writing. Film has frequently been used to present large quantities of reading material.

The pacing of the material is a significant factor here. An individual's reading speed is calculated in words per minute, and it is possible to work out an exact rate at which writing is displayed on the screen. A pre-test of students, using mechanical pacers, could establish an average reading rate, and the material in the television programmes could begin at this rate, and gradually speed up the rate of display, forcing the viewer to hurry through the material, without rereadings. There are two objections to using this procedure. First, speed in reading is only important relative to comprehension. Second, every competent reader uses a variety of reading speeds, and reading skills, according to the nature of the material, and his own particular requirements. A section in an encyclopaedia might be read slowly and carefully, if the reader wished to absorb what it was about; it might be skimmed through if the reader was in search of a particular point. We skim through a dictionary to find the entry we want; we then might read it all carefully, or ignore the classification and look at the definition, or vice versa. Closely argued nonfiction we will tend to read more slowly than an informal biography; a biography packed with detailed dates and incidents will need closer scrutiny. Fictional works have different styles, some requiring slower reading than others. Accurately to gauge the different speeds at which certain material could be read is out of the question. An individual with a mechanical pacer can adjust the speed to the material and his own ability; the resulting rate in words per minute then describes his achievement for that particular piece of writing. We cannot then use that rate as a prescriptive formula for all material with any accuracy at all. Nonetheless, we can approximate the speed of presentation, very roughly, according to the type of writing, and the type of comprehension we are aiming at. We might attempt a stylistic analysis, on the basis of word-count, and structure complexity, though any criteria we use would be subjective. Pre-testing will give a rough guide as to the rate at which to expose a particular type of material. However, the key factor in pacing material lies in the type of comprehension exercises we expect the reader to undertake.

We read to obtain information. Sometimes this information is easily understood, if the written material is in a clear style, clearly set out, and our ability to recognize structures and graphological features is adequate. Understanding also depends upon our general intelligence, education and maturity. Even given all these factors, some written material is hard to understand. The information is not readily available: the text requires an interpretation of some kind. Rail and air timetables require interpretation, according to our own requirements; reports in some newspapers require interpretation, according to the political bias of the journal; hard-sell advertisements require careful interpretation; different reports of the same event will require an interpretation, if we are to know what actually occurred. Comprehension questions on written material need to cover both types of understanding—information and interpretation. At this level, we do not require a structured response, necessarily. We may ask for single words; the number of a correct answer from a list; the choice of the correct picture; sometimes there will be no one interpretation, and we may ask the learner to produce his own. Questions and answers may be verbal or written.

When asking the reader for information from a passage of writing, memory is an important factor to bear in mind. In some types of material—biographical details, recipes, posters, catalogues, lists of various kinds—we might ask the reader for one or two points of information to look out for in a passage which he subsequently reads. Such passages can be shown fairly rapidly, the questions repeated, perhaps in multiple-choice form, and time allowed for a response. In passages of logical argument, in anecdotes, descriptions, or instructions, questions may be asked after the passage is read. In this case, the question should be contextualized as much as possible in the multiple-choice answers. The use of alternative pictures may provide such contexts more simply than written or spoken words. Response to questions asking for an interpretation is more difficult to arrange. This type of material is best presented together with follow-up facilities, either in ancillary notes, or classroom discussion. This is particularly important when the material is derived from other subject areas in a school curriculum. Written questions in algebra or geometry ('If x equals 2, and y equals 5 . . .') will require longer periods of time to interpret than can be incorporated in a television programme. Three or four different reports of a road accident will need discussion in class before an interpretation can be reached. On the other hand, the interpretation of timetables, graphs, or charts might be done in the TV programme itself, with the presentation of a choice of possible interpretations from which the viewer has to select one.

Television, then, can be of assistance in the teaching of the reading skill, though it is unlikely that any teaching system will require the medium to handle the quantity of practice material that is required. Large stretches of written material on the screen is a waste of television time, and cannot possibly handle the varied demands, intelligence and pace of the many viewers. In the early stages of reading, television's strength is in the procedures for letter and word recognition. It can draw attention to significant features, and present a large number of examples very rapidly. In the later stages of reading, its strength lies in the presentation of the wide range of written material which the learner is likely to meet. Provision can be made in other sections of the teaching system for narrative prose and textbooks of various kinds, both in print and in type. These items constitute standard school equipment. But hard-pressed teachers may find it hard to bring to the classroom all the other types of written material which are available, which the student meets outside the classroom, and which can all help to reinforce what he learns from formal instruction. As with the speaking and listening skills, television's major contribution to the reading skill, especially at the advanced level, is to bring in the outside world.

Notes

1. Marshall McLuhan: *Understanding Media* Sphere Books 1967, p. 91
2. Joyce Morris: *Standards and Progress in Reading* NFER 1966
3. Edward Fry: *Teaching Faster Reading* Cambridge University Press 1963, p. 15
4. M. Macmillan: *Efficiency in Reading ETIC*, British Council 1965, p. 17
5. L. A. Hill and J. M. Ure: *English Sounds and Spellings* Oxford University Press 1962
6. Harvey N. Perlish: 'Early Reading via Television' *E.T.I.* Vol. 4 No. 2 1970
7. David E. Eskey: 'Advanced Reading: The Structural Problem' *Forum* Vol. IX No. 5 1971
8. Richard Sherrington: 'A Television Course in Faster Reading for Ethiopia' *E.T.I.* Vol. 1 No. 2 1967
9. C. C. Fries: *Linguistics and Reading* Holt, Rinehart and Winston 1963

8 Television and the Writing Skill

Superficially, it seems odd to mention the electronic medium of television and the ancient art of writing in the same sentence. To suggest that the passive mass medium could help to teach the highly individualistic creative act of writing would be strange, were it not for the fact that this very object has been successfully attempted in a number of countries. In Italy, Jamaica, Uganda, and elsewhere, television programmes have dealt with various aspects of the writing skill, from basic letter formation to the art of good letter-writing. Of all the four categories of language skill, writing is by far the most difficult for the native-user of the language to accomplish satisfactorily. The enormous field of literary criticism is evidence of the fact that we tend to judge the writing skill far more severely than any other language activity. Nor does this critical faculty restrict itself to literature. The schools of journalism, the number of books on good letter-writing, correspondence, and the art of the concise memorandum, all indicate that good writing is an elite occupation. Far more difficult is it, therefore, for the second-language learner to achieve even an adequate mastery of the skill. How absurd it is to expect him to express himself in a creative composition upon the subject of his happiest moment, or a day by the sea. The importance of individual taste in writing is further demonstrated by the diversity of theories on the best way to teach the skill. Authors become very dogmatic over such subjects as neatness of presentation, the value of copying, or dictation exercises; whether students should begin to form printed letter shapes, or start with connected writing; which system of handwriting should be enforced in schools, or whether handwriting is so related to character development that it is best not taught at all. Such discussions invariably avoid the main concern of the student. In the vast majority of cases, he does not wish to learn to write as he might learn to paint; his writing will be specifically functional. Initially, his writing will be aimed at reinforcing other language work.[1] This has traditionally been the attitude adopted to the writing skill, and has led to over-emphasis of such activities as written translation, dictation, and the laborious writing out of grammatical exercises. Important though such functions may be, they are not an end in themselves. The teaching system will need to specify the type of writing activity the students are likely to require outside the classroom. The course has then to be graded to help them achieve an adequate performance in these activities.

Problems of Using Television

Students cannot write in groups, as they can speak, listen and read in groups; it is the most individual of the language skills, and requires more individual teaching than the others. Yet the teaching of writing, like the other language skills, is basically a question of initial demonstration by the teacher and subsequent practice by the student. The individual teaching is then a matter of dealing with each student's difficulties. These may be physical, in the early stages: an inability to perceive small differences in letter shapes, or an inability to form shapes, space them correctly, or keep them in a straight line. The teacher in the classroom obviously has to handle these problems. Television can play a part at the stage of demonstration, both of the actual forming of letter shapes, and of the finished product. To begin, it may be necessary to teach students to hold a pen in the most convenient way to form English letters. This is particularly important for students familiar with writing Chinese, or Arabic characters. Television can demonstrate this in a big close-up whereas the teacher will have to show each student individually. The television teacher can use a variety of devices for demonstration purposes, from the blackboard to the overhead projector. Alternatively, the camera can take shots from a mirror angled above the television teacher as he writes at a desk. The students should be encouraged to copy the television teacher during the programme itself. This will allow the classroom teacher to move from student to student, checking on each individual, as the demonstration is in progress. For the home student, the television demonstration should be closely related to ancillary material. The book might show a letter shape, with arrows showing how it is formed. Difficult to follow by itself, it can be demonstrated by the television teacher, who used the book illustration itself as the basis for his demonstration. The accompanying book is then a permanent and clear record, which the home student can use in his subsequent practice. The most important part of the writing instruction comes after the television programme, when the student practises by himself. The integration of the programmes into the total teaching system has to be complete. In the Italian literacy series, 'It's never too late', the lesson consisted of a half-hour preparation, a half-hour TV programme, and an hour's practice.[2] Each TV programme used a variety of techniques, designed to entertain as well as teach, and was also teaching the reading skill. The amount of actual demonstration of writing in the programme was, therefore, relatively small; it was intended that the main effort here should be made in the subsequent practice session. Nonetheless the student spent part of the programme copying the shapes being produced by the television teacher, while background music was played. It is not every TV station which can allow airtime for such time-consuming activities, and it is more likely that demonstration of this nature will be quite short. It is all the more important, therefore, that they should be clearly related to method and textbook being used by the student in the classroom, or at home. Decisions need to be made for the whole teaching scheme: writing style; connected or printed; shape formation, letter formation or whole-word formation. It does not then matter how short the television demonstration is, since it will relate precisely to the instruction received elsewhere in the system.

Sound to Symbol

To begin, writing will be an adjunct to other language skills. The phonological aspect of writing is important in helping students to recognize symbol-to-sound relationships. The student hears a sound, repeats it himself, and writes down the letter which corresponds to it. Where the one-to-one relationship does not apply, the student may be encouraged to perform the same operation with whole words. He may be helped by being given words with blank spaces which he must fill in himself. These activities depend upon the student's ability to recognize sounds and letters correctly. A simple story might be presented on television, using film, pictures, or written words. In each case, the story is also told on the sound-track. At certain points, a word which emphasizes a particular phonic problem is isolated; it may be shown with letters missing; there may be a visual cue of some kind to draw attention to the word being spoken. It is repeated and the student asked to write down the word he hears. Space should be provided in his notebook for him to do this. When he has completed this exercise, the written word is shown to confirm his writing. Minimal pairs (*bull*/*ball*), consonant clusters (*clock*/*desks*), and so on, can be incorporated into the story, and students asked to write them down, or to fill in the crucial letters where the framework is printed in the students' book. The student should be encouraged to repeat the word he hears before writing it, to confirm his recognition of the correct sound. Television stories might embody a large number of elements in which writing will assist the viewer to practise sound-to-symbol relationships. At the end of such a story, the student may have written down a set of words, such as *ele**ph**ant*/*tele**ph**one*/**f**ur/**fi**ne*; **c**at/**c**heese/**c**ity*; **y**ellow/**fl**y/*pretty*. Having finished the story, the viewer's attention can be drawn to those letters which appear in each word in the set, and demonstrate how their sound-values change in each word. Such an exercise gives practice in all the skills, and can be done fairly rapidly.

Letter formation

The actual formation of graphic symbols might begin with simple shapes, separated or joined; it might begin with the letters themselves, categorized according to their use of lines, curves, and a mixture of both; it might begin with writing whole words. Later it will be necessary to give particular practice to likely areas of confusion: $n/m/h$; $b/d/p/q$; *that/what*; *these/those*; and so on. This early practice usually begins with simply copying, which is a useful procedure both for recognition of letter and word shapes, and for demonstrating the formation of letters. The students can watch the shapes being formed by the television teacher, in big close-up, while the teacher moves round the classroom helping individuals. The shapes can be made to appear on the screen by means of animation techniques, but it is probably more useful for the students to actually see a hand forming the shapes. Care must be taken not to let the hand obscure the shapes, and the pacing of the demonstration is important.[3] Viewers should be encouraged to make pen strokes without hesitation, and this can be assisted by pacing the television demonstration fairly briskly. Initially, this may cause problems, but it will compel the viewers to attempt to emulate the speed of the television teacher, rather than spending too long over each shape, as is frequently the case when copying from the blackboard. The great advantage of using television here is the freedom which it gives the teacher to concentrate on his pupils, and keep the copying speed at the same rate as the television teacher's. Beginning with single shapes, or letters, and pausing after each very briefly, the TV teacher can then move on to two, three or four shapes or letters in a row for the viewers to copy. The second stage is that of reproduction. Here, the shape, letter or word is demonstrated on the screen while the viewers watch; it is then removed, and a picture (or a blank screen) displayed while the students write down the shape from memory. With single letters, the screen might go blank for two or three seconds between each exposure. It may not be necessary to show the letter actually being formed, but simply to present it for the viewers to see and write down. With words, the viewers will need longer to perceive the item to be copied, and longer to write it down. A related picture and background music might fill in these pauses. The correct form might be shown after each pause for writing, or at the end of a short sequence. This enables the viewers to check through what they have written. Pacing is again important. Pre-tests with a representative audience sample can help establish a reasonable speed which should be aimed at by all viewers. Alternatively, a group of students can be brought into the studio to participate in the programmes, as was done in the Italian series. This can act as an encouragement to the viewers, and can be a most useful guide for the pacing and grading of the writing material to be copied and reproduced during the programme.

The Production of Written Structures

At the early stage of forming letter shapes, and relating spellings to sounds, the available television time can be used quite efficiently for simple demonstrations and simultaneous copying and reproduction by the students. Much more practice will be required of course, outside television time, but, because the units are small, a television demonstration can cover a good deal of ground in a relatively short time. When we move on to the level of structure, however, the units of language to be written are longer, and television becomes far less efficient as a means of teaching writing. It is a waste of airtime to wait for viewers to write out whole sentences, or even whole sense groups. The other elements in the teaching system have to take the major load. As with the reading skill, the structure syllabus for the writing skill will have to emphasize those elements peculiar to the written form of language. Writing tends to be more formal, both in content and in layout, and this can be practised from the very beginning of 'meaningful' writing. The functional aspect of writing can also be emphasized early on, as is the case in many literacy programmes. Students should begin by writing their names and addresses. Regular writing practice can be provided by writing the days of the week, the date, or daily information such as the weather, the subject of each lesson, and so on. These activities can be included in a televised course with the help of ancillary notes; the students can fill in this daily data in their books, or on the classroom blackboard, before the TV lesson; reference can then be made to it at the beginning of each TV lesson, checking spelling, layout, and the information content itself. The writing of sentence patterns should all begin with blank-filling exercises, provided in the student's book. A televised story might be interrupted with a question, relating to a numbered incomplete answer in the student's book. The question might be asked in the sound channel, or in words written on the screen, depending upon the viewers' skill in listening and reading comprehension. Alternatively instructions can be given before the story, asking the viewer to fill in the blanks in the sentences when he is given a numbered visual or verbal cue. For example, a character in the story might be looking for a book. The picture cuts to the book behind a vase of flowers; the teacher says, 'Question number one'; the viewer finds question number one in his book, which reads, 'The book is . . . the vase.' He then has to write in the word 'behind', before the story proceeds. Blank-filling might be extended to simple substitution exercises, where the viewer is asked to cross out incorrect words in a sense group, and write in the correct words. In the example just given, the picture of the book behind the vase might be related to a sentence in the student's book which reads, 'The book is in front of the bag.' He then has to cross out the incorrect words, and substitute *behind* and *vase*. At an advanced stage, the student might be asked to perform simple transformations upon material written in his workbook. The televised story may concern the adventures of a group of boys; they might be shown running through a rainstorm. The teacher then asks the viewers to change a sentence in their books, which reads, 'The boy, who wasn't wearing a raincoat, got wet.' The viewer must then pluralize the sentence, by crossing out wrong forms and writing in correct forms. Or, at another point in the story, the viewers might be asked to make a question from a sentence which reads, 'They go to school everyday.' Help may be given by providing incomplete answers. Although time-consuming when carried out during the TV transmission itself, these exercises can introduce a whole series of substitution and transformation exercises on the same pattern, which the student has to complete after the TV programme. These extra exercises can be based upon the televised story, thus contextualizing what would otherwise be a random drill sequence. Again, the act of crossing out words and making corrections is not conducive to fine handwriting; at this level, however, we are concerned with the ability to write down correct structural forms and not with a well-formed style.

Dictation is another technique which can be successfully used from a television screen. Particular phonic problems can be pointed by asking students to write down a word spoken from the screen: *ship* for example, as opposed to *sheep*. When the student has been given time for this, the correct spelling with the appropriate picture can be shown. Sentences can be dictated in sense groups, and the students then asked to punctuate them correctly. At a later stage, a programme might end with a whole story read to the viewers. The same story will be written out in their workbooks, with certain words omitted, according to their contribution to the sentence structure, and their inherent difficulties of spelling. The story can be read to the accompaniment of visuals of some kind; the students' books should be closed. When the programme is over, the students open their books, and read through the story, filling in the missing items from memory. Corrections can either be made by the classroom teacher, by printing the passage in full elsewhere in the student's book, or by using it for reading practice in the next television programme.

As we have seen, the writing skill, at the level of symbol formation and structure, is closely related to the other language skills. To spell correctly, the student has to recognize the word forms, or read, correctly. This skill is assisted by his ability to recognize sounds and relate them to written symbols. When considering how to spell a new word, the student will tend to pronounce it out loud, in order to apply a generalization he has made from previously acquired data. Writing helps to confirm our knowledge of the other language skills, and to practise them, since written contexts of language use are more readily available to us than verbal contexts; they are easier to control and observe. Sooner or later, however, the writing skill has to take off on its own, to begin to tackle those functional requirements of writing which the student will need. He cannot be expected to leap into report writing, or letter composition, to write up chemistry experiments, or take notes at a lecture, on the basis of the writing he has accomplished in consolidating his other language skills. Unlike speech, with its allowance for hesitation phenomena, incomplete structures, and its need to respond instantly to a variety of stimuli, writing requires far more formal control. This is true for the native-user, as well as the second-language learner. This formal control has to be taught, so that the written communication is as clear as possible to the reader. Each type of written material has its own style and forms but all writing needs to contain clear connections from thought to thought, from sentence to sentence, from paragraph to paragraph. We need to discuss this form of written material before going on to talk about content.

Guided Composition

Formal control of writing is encouraged in a number of language courses by guided composition techniques. Sometimes these are in the form of sense group frames. Each frame contains a choice of items, which may be put together in various ways to form a logical, connected passage. To begin, any choice from the frames will yield a correct passage of writing; students can simply write down any item from each frame in sequence, and they will arrive at a satisfactory composition. Later, the choices in the frames may depend upon structural criteria. For example, the choice of an initial noun-form will dictate the choice of the following pronouns; having selected one type of time-phrase, the student has to select the appropriate verb-form which follows. Later still, the choices in the frames may be semantic, rather than structural. A story which begins with a man putting on heavy boots may proceed to a choice between the man diving into the sea or beginning to climb a mountain. An early choice between a tailor, a grocer, or a butcher, will entail later choices between cutting cloth, delivering eggs, and weighing meat. Alternatively, formal control over written material is sometimes presented in the form of serial questions; in writing out the full answers to each question in sequence, the student puts together a connected passage. Here, the connections might be structural or semantic. Again, sentences are sometimes presented in a jumbled form—descriptions of changing a tyre, or boiling an egg, for example—and students are asked to sort out the logical ordering of events and write out a clear passage.

Television is well-suited to this kind of formal control. Its life-blood is material clearly presented in script or on film to achieve maximum communication. Even unscripted interviews have to be sequenced and controlled by skilled interviewers. Television's normal means of communication has simply to be broken down, and emphasized in places, to provide material for the viewer-learner. The actual writing will have to be done, for the most part, after the television programme is finished. Clear links with the viewer's workbook must be demonstrated; it might contain serial questions, passages with blanks to fill in, or frames of various kinds. The television presentation must relate to the type of exercise precisely. Writing at its most controlled level might be handled as follows. A story presents two boys who find a wallet and a hat. Each boy takes one of the objects and goes through six or seven actions to attempt to locate the owner. We have two storylines, presented one after the other. At each stage in the action, the frame is frozen, and the number of the action in the sequence is shown, plus a key-word—perhaps the verb-form. Alternatively, a caption could be shown at each stage with this information. The last caption in each story tabulates the sequence of events. The stories themselves may be told in full dialogue. The student's workbook contains a composition frame which sets out the two stories in report form. This may be in the past tense, or the present-perfect tense (ending 'He hasn't found the owner yet'). Each box in the composition frame contains identical structural forms for the two stories, plus a third story. Thus: FRAME 1 —*He.* FRAME 2—*found/picked up/discovered.* FRAME 3—*a wallet/a hat/a pound note.* And so on. The student has followed the televised story, and has been shown the sequence of events which used the key-words which also appear in his composition frame. After the programme, he has to write out both stories from his frame, plus a third.

A similar format might be used to demonstrate a structural sequence which depends upon the correct choice of relative pronoun and subsequent clause. Again, the sequence of events has to be clearly shown—for example, a chemistry experiment— and numbered together with key-words or phrases. The student's book might contain a number of questions, the answers to which will, in sequence, produce the account of the experiment. Gradually, these formal controls can be withdrawn, so that the student-viewer is encouraged to make his own sequential connections; the sentences in his workbook might be presented in a jumbled fashion, or the composition frame might demand semantic selection at each stage. It is then only his memory of the televised presentation which will enable him to write out the correctly sequenced passage. At a later stage, the television programme can include discussion of a story sequence, between the television teacher and a group of participants. The beginning of a story might be shown. Then there is discussion about possible developments of the story. For example, a man has to take some medicine to a hospital in London very urgently. Perhaps he loses the medicine; perhaps his car breaks down; perhaps he loses his way. These alternatives can be discussed and the story can continue in these three ways. Each story then has further branching-off points which require discussion, before selection. This kind of treatment can be related to material set out in the student's book. They must write out the story, following the decisions discussed in the programme, and then continue the story to a conclusion. Other visual material might be used for discussion purposes, such as graphs, or charts of various kinds. A report can then be put together during the programme, using sentences which have to be completed. For example, 'In 1964, Germany exported *x* million cars', can be duplicated, with a number of substitutions in various places, from the graph. Conclusions can then be drawn about increases and decreases in exports in various countries over a period of time. A similar graph and questions can be incorporated into the student's book. A series of conditional sentences can be strung together from perusal of a plane timetable and concluding suggestions made about the quickest, most convenient way of travelling from place A to place B. Again, further examples of the same type of writing material can be put into accompanying workbooks.

The content of the writing exercises should, as far as is possible, tend towards the functional requirements of the students. Where English is a medium of instruction in schools, copious use should be made of information and styles from other subject areas. Writing should be restricted to facts and descriptions for the second-language learner; he should not be asked to express his ideas, since this presents an opportunity to attempt an unformed, literary style, likely to do more harm than good. Descriptions of science experiments can be attempted, after a television demonstration, enumerating each stage in turn, and drawing attention to the passive form to be adopted in the account. Descriptions of geological formations, features of weather, distillations of comparative temperature charts, historical accounts, brief biographies: all these can be presented clearly and interestingly on television, and related to composition forms, controlled to varying degrees, in the student's workbook. Where specific formats are required for reports of various kinds, this can be demonstrated by actually writing it out on an overhead projector during the programme, or presenting a finished report for reading practice. This is particularly useful with regard to letter-writing, in which the form of layout is important. Demonstration of letter format can be presented as a prelude to the student's practice after the programme, using material from his book.

Note-taking

A situation can be televised in which a secretary, or a student, is taking notes from a lecture, or from written material. This is the basis of précis work, and is an extremely useful writing skill, requiring considerable practice. To begin, the student can be given the notes which summarize a film commentary that he hears in the television programme. A similar film and commentary can then be presented, with built-in pauses at places where a note needs to be made. This time, the student may be presented with incomplete notes which he must fill in. Practice can be continued over several programmes until the student has sufficient confidence to make his own notes. The second half of this technique is to write up the notes into an acceptable form. To begin, this exercise might simply be a question of extending contracted forms (*I've*, *doesn't*) into the full written forms. Later, the notes might be extended to simple sentences (*hot air rises—moves to land— clouds form*); lastly, these simple sentences can be expanded by using conjunctions suggested in the students' book. In addition to notes made on heard language, the course may contain note-taking from material which is presented on a roller-caption for purposes of reading practice. The viewer may be asked to note down three or four crucial points from a passage he reads from the TV screen, and write them up into a short summary as an exercise. This may be as straightforward as noting down dates, places and times from a newspaper report of a royal visit. Notes can take many forms, from the newspaper report or film commentary, to the simple, 'Dinner in oven, back in five minutes.' Students will want to be able to decipher both forms, and to write both forms.

Writing requires much more thought and consideration than the other language skills. Much material is rewritten several times before it appears in print. It is hard to write down exactly what you want to say without spending time on it. For this reason, an instant medium like television, which cannot be wound back like a film, has little to offer the learner-writer. It can provide demonstration; it can show the contexts in which the many writing activities take place; it can provide the stimulus for writing activity. But the activity itself remains almost entirely an off-screen business. Television has proved its usefulness in teaching writing at the very early stage, and at the advanced stage of discussion and analysis. The great bulk of writing activity, however, lies between these extremes, and television has little to offer here which other elements in the teaching system cannot provide more effectively.

Notes

1. Wilga M. Rivers: *Teaching Foreign-Language Skills* University of Chicago Press 1968
2. Maria Grazia Puglisi: 'Television and the Fight against Illiteracy' *EBU Review* Nov. 1963
3. G. Grimmett and B. Kirby: 'Showing handwriting on the Television Screen' *E.T.I.* Vol. 4 No. 1 March 1970

9 Linking the Studio and the Learner

We have now completed an inventory of English language skills, and the possible ways of using television in each, at each level of difficulty. A televised course in teaching English will now be based upon decisions made as to the type of synthesis we wish to produce from the inventory. It is possible that a total teaching scheme will employ TV for only one type of skill at one level of difficulty—letter formation, listening comprehension, or reading of sense-groups. All other language skills in such a synthesis would be handled by other elements in the scheme—the teacher, textbook, tapes, and so on. It is possible that television might be asked to take on the entire English-teaching course, teaching all skills at all levels. Neither of these extreme forms of course construction is practical or likely. Television is only efficient if employed for broad educational purposes; it is clearly a waste of expensive airtime to concentrate on one part of one skill at one level of difficulty. However, if television is being broadly used to teach a number of subjects in the curriculum, the airtime allotted to English might be employed for such a specific purpose, without impairing the efficiency of the educational television system. At the other extreme, it is very unlikely that any television system will have sufficient airtime to provide the intensive and extensive programming that a total English course would require. There will always be the need for selection and the consequent need for ancillary material of some kind. The role of television in the synthesized English course will normally lie somewhere between these two extremes.

Decisions on the synthesis itself will depend upon two factors. First, the availability of various teaching means. This includes adequately-trained teachers; the adequate supply and distribution facilities of textbooks, tapes, records; the adequate provision of simple classroom aids such as blackboard, chalk, and other graphics materials. Second, the chosen synthesis will depend upon the type and situation of the learner; his motivation, his immediate learning environment, whether his learning is supervised or not. We cannot place television in our teaching scheme without knowing something of these factors, and making provision for them. Effective teaching is a two-way business, though some subjects require student feedback less than others. Language teaching relies heavily upon the kind of feedback which is available to the teacher in his classroom. This becomes crucial when the student works alone, and when he uses a textbook, tape, record, radio or TV. Experiment has verified the common-sense notion that the communication of information is most satisfactory where the receiving end is organized; where there are teachers or monitors to follow up one-way instruction with face-to-face reinforcement.[1] Where there are no such facilities, it is even more important to make extra provision for the receiving end of the communication. In either case, there have to be organized links between one end of the communication and the other—between the television studio and the individual learner. In this section, we shall discuss these links; we can then go on, in the concluding section, to talk about the types of television course and programme format which might be attempted.

Supervised and Non-supervised Learners

We can usefully classify potential learners into two groups; those who might be in a school system, or evening classes, and whose instruction is normally in the hands of a classroom teacher or monitor; and those who study at home by themselves. To class these groups as 'captive' and 'non-captive' is misleading, since it implies differences in motivation which may not be helpful. The student of the Open University, for example, may be better motivated to use television in his home than the student in the classroom. It is easier to classify these groups as 'supervised' and 'non-supervised', since the presence or absence of an intermediary intructor between studio and student is of enormous importance.

Supervised instruction then covers the child who learns from the domestic television set, in the company of his mother. Non-supervised instruction then includes the school class who are told to watch television because there are no teachers available to look after them. In terms of these two groups, we can further analyse the studio-student link into three sections. The first section is concerned with setting up the link, dealing with the organizational problems of fitting television into a total teaching system. This is the stage of INTEGRATION. The second section deals with the television programme itself, and the problem of involving the participation of the learner who is watching it. This is the stage of RESPONSE. The last section of the link is that of ASSESSMENT: did the programme teach what it set out to teach? How effective was the communication, and where did it break down?

Integration: The Supervised Learner

Where instruction is supervised, the establishment of a link between studio and student depends to a very large extent upon the quality of the supervisor. Where he is a skilled English language teacher, the television course writer can rely upon him for a number of functions; where he is simply a class supervisor—a monitor as opposed to teacher—the television teaching can afford to be much more direct. Whatever the quality of the teacher or monitor, he must be informed of his role in the studio-student link, and trained accordingly. This type of orientation training may be done at the teacher-training institute, or by short in-service courses for practising teachers. Television must be presented as part of a teaching system, which is not in competition with the supervisor, but which is of use to him, just as he is of use to it. He must know what the television will do in the teaching scheme, and what he must do, before, during and after the programme. He should be given practice in running a television lesson, or, if this is not possible, be given demonstrations, perhaps in television programmes aimed at the supervisors themselves. Again where possible, he should be made aware of the possibilities and limitations of television in teaching English, invited to the studio, asked for his suggestions, made to feel that the television programme, like he himself, is part of an overall teaching scheme.

The supervisor, and the director of the institute in which he operates, need to be aware of the importance of the physical and organizational elements of the receiving situation. Arrangements need to be made for the siting of the TV set in the classroom, and the seating arrangements of the viewers themselves; the installation of the antenna, and the arrangements made for servicing facilities. The television programme schedules have to be made out well in advance of the institution's academic year, so that they can be incorporated into the school timetable. It is rarely possible to arrange for all schoolchildren in a country to watch the same programme at the same time of day; a workable arrangement has to be made between school and television authorities, so that there is a balance between the possible number of repeat transmissions and the need to juggle with each school timetable. Directors will want to know whether to allocate one classroom to a TV receiver, and move classes about the building during the day; or whether to have a TV set on a mobile stand, and have antennae connections in a number of classrooms. The length of the TV programme, and how its timing relates to the timing of the school lesson, will have to be worked out. Will there be two TV lessons to one classroom lesson? Can the TV station go off the air, or transmit continuity slides and music between transmissions, to allow for the teacher's preparation and follow-up? If not, will there be time between the two TV lessons for the mobile TV set, or the classes, to be moved about the building? Is the continuity music to be heard during the teacher's preparation; if so, is it of a type not to distract his students? Such minutiae are important to the individual supervisor, and the hard-pressed director. The television authority's attitude to them may condition the attitude of the receiving institution. They are all an essential part of the preparation stage of the studio-student link.

The presence of a supervisor makes it easier for the television course writer to know his audience. Where there is organized instruction, there is a rough guide to the age and ability range of the viewing students, since they will have been streamed in some way for the institute's own purposes. A television format can then be geared to the interests of children in elementary or secondary levels, to evening classes aimed at particular types of adult audience—immigrants, tourists, generally interested viewers, and so on. Where there is no supervisor, the writer of a television course is compelled to make gross assumptions about the type of audience he is likely to get; his programmes, and his ancillary material, are likely to be unsatisfactory for many viewers for whom his assumptions are not true. A supervisor's presence can limit the number of assumptions which have to be made simply because individual viewers are categorized into groups for the supervisor's benefit. The assumptions are even fewer where the categories are on a national basis, as in a state educational system. Communication from student to studio is also facilitated if the students are represented by a supervisor, who can more easily, and more successfully, keep the studio informed of the type of learner, his needs and how far the television programmes are satisfying them. The mass medium is compelled to treat its audiences as types, not individuals, and a supervised educational environment enables the programme producer to make more accurate definitions of each type.

In an ideal systems approach to the teaching of English, the introduction of television would involve the immediate revision of the entire syllabus, so that the various tasks could be efficiently allotted to the different elements in the system. Televised instruction and the syllabus would then be interlocked, with no danger of duplication of effort. This ideal situation is unlikely to be the case. Even where television is introduced at critical moments of curriculum reform, there are no textbooks on the market which allot certain activities to other media. The reform would have to take the expensive path of specially written books for a certain country with a certain type of educational television network with a known airtime availability. The problems of introducing television into an existing, workable syllabus are complex, if duplication is to be avoided, and television is to be of real value. From our inventory of the uses of television in teaching English we can decide what we want the new medium to do. Whatever we decide on this issue, it will not succeed unless it is clear to everyone—scriptwriter, supervisor and student—where television fits into the existing syllabus and classroom practice. In the preparatory stage of linking studio to student, the relationship of TV programme to syllabus is of vital importance.

Where the syllabus employed in supervised classes is viable, and produces results, television has to slot neatly into classroom practice with minimum disruption. Depending upon the quality of the teacher handling the syllabus, television might introduce new work, or it might be used to practise work already introduced by the supervisor. Alternatively, television might be employed to handle one particular language-teaching task—one which is most difficult for the supervisor to handle. This will depend upon the availability of classroom facilities. Television might concentrate on reading, where there are no supplementary readers, and no duplication equipment. It might concentrate on speech practice, using native English speakers. The grading of material used in the television series will have to follow precisely that of the recognized syllabus. Pacing is somewhat more difficult. Certain textbook courses conveniently break up the teacher's work into week-by-week activity; pacing is thus dictated to the teacher and the television course writer. Other textbooks, divided into chapters or units, are provided to the teacher with the instruction that a certain number of sections should be completed by the end of the year. His weekly pacing of material then depends upon his own decisions about his students' capabilities. A television course, in this situation, has to dictate the pace of instruction. It cannot fit in with each individual teacher—the teacher has to fit in with the television course. It will be necessary to look into previous classroom practice with a particular course, and come to some generally agreeable compromise before establishing the pace of the television series. Where the television programmes are fully integrated into an existing syllabus and textbook, it will not be necessary to produce ancillary material, except in so far as the supervisor needs to be informed of the exact role of television in the syllabus, and his own part in the utilization of the programmes. In a televised course in speech practice, it may be thought advisable to provide tapes or records to classrooms, but these, too, will relate directly to the textbook course which the teacher is using.

A problem arises for television programmes aimed at supervised classes where the syllabus in use is either non-existent or weak. Television is compelled to fit in with what already exists, rather than attempt to strike out on its own, since the latter course can only lead to confusion in the classroom. Ideally, the introduction of television into an organized educational system would go hand in hand with syllabus development, revised textbooks, and upgraded teachers. This ideal aim is rarely achieved —one element in development normally precedes the others. Where this one element is television, it becomes necessary to bring all other elements in the system into line with the organization of the television programmes. Rather than limiting the role of television to supporting an unsuitable textbook and classroom methodology, the television system should be given first place, and the unsuitable textbook and syllabus allotted a supplementary role. In effect, this means writing a total syllabus, complete with full teachers' notes, students' books, and using any other supplementary facilities which are available. Television then takes its rightful place as one element in the system. The outmoded textbook which is being used in schools is not discarded; attempts are made to incorporate material from it in the total course. It no longer dictates the grading and pacing of the syllabus—this is the prerogative of the television course writer —but it is used only when it has something useful to contribute. Again, the teacher has to be aware of the place of his textbook in the total scheme, and the educational authorities must sanction the use of a syllabus based upon the televised course. Hopefully, this will be a temporary measure. Later, a concerted attempt at curriculum reform and textbook revision may be undertaken, in which case, the television programmes will be adjusted to fit in with the revised scheme.

In discussing a possible teaching synthesis for supervised instruction, the following general points seem to hold. The stronger the syllabus, the better the textbook, and the more qualified the teachers themselves, the more restricted a television course can afford to be. Its role can be limited, and the type of instruction it provides can be more intensive. The weaker the syllabus and the quality of the teachers, the more extensive the role of the television course. The course writer will have to provide more ancillary material for students and teachers, and adopt a more direct approach in his presentation of the material.

Integration: The Non-supervised Learner

We can now move on to a discussion of the integration stage of the studio-student link, where instruction is not supervised. This situation applies to all broadcasting authorities which mainly transmit entertainment and information programmes, and which decide to put out language-teaching programmes for the general public. In all such broadcasting, assumptions have to be made about the taste and viewing habits of the potential audience. These assumptions may be informed hypotheses, based upon extensive audience research, door-to-door surveys, sample interviewing in depth. Very often, however, they are simply assumptions based upon subjective opinion. Nonetheless, if the aim is to win an audience, and retain their interest long enough for them to learn something, a number of vital factors have to be considered. To begin, the scheduling of the programmes, and the number of repeat transmissions, have to be based upon information about the working habits of the potential audience. Will sufficient people be prepared to get up early to watch programmes before they go to work? Are people generally too tired for late-night teaching programmes? Is early evening the best compromise, or do most people eat supper at that time? How far does such timing conflict with other broadcasting demands, such as children's television? It is easy to avoid such problems by assuming that people will watch if they want to learn, and that they won't watch if they don't, irrespective of the time of day. But the motivational problems of the unsupervised learner are not so easily dismissed. Few houses have more than one receiver, and it is normally placed in the social centre of the house. Domestic activities will distract the lone learner, however well motivated he may be. Allowance has to be made for attention lapses when the programmes are written—they have to possess 'built-in redundancy'. Nothing will be learnt during the first few minutes where there is no supervisor to focus the learner's attention and prepare him for the programme. There must be far more repetition and recapitulation in the programmes for the unsupervised learner than where there is a teacher to carry out follow-up work. In certain situations, the teaching 'pill' will have to be heavily sugared if the audience is to be attracted at all, and this necessarily limits the time available for straight instruction. In many countries, unsupervised viewing is not done at home, but in communal places such as restaurants or on the street. Television programming cannot be contemplated until something is known of the situation into which the programmes are likely to be projected.

Similarly, assumptions have to be made about the type of audience aimed at. It is not enough to classify the course itself for beginners, near-beginners, or advanced students of English, on a take-it-or-leave-it basis. Such labels are unhelpful to potential viewers who cannot be expected to categorize themselves. Some attempt has to be made to find out the potential audience for a language programme, and plan both programmes and supplementary material accordingly. Where programmes to unsupervised learners are complementing a correspondence course—as is the case with Open University students—something is known of the educational background of the viewers. In England, it is possible to make some assumptions about a French-language teaching series and its possible audience, because of the place which French teaching has in the English school curriculum. One can expect a rudimentary knowledge of French, which one could not assume with Russian, say. In either case, it is necessary to conduct a preliminary survey, to establish guidelines concerning the audience and their previous knowledge. Two or three pilot programmes might be run, with information about the course and available supplementary material, and asking interested viewers to write in, or fill in a published questionnaire, with details of themselves and their language background. Such a procedure would provide a rough guide for the course writer, and go some way to bridging the enormous gap between the studio and the unsupervised viewer-learner.

Language programmes for unsupervised learners are most effective where they are connected closely to an existing correspondence course.[2] In many countries, correspondence sections of universities or colleges employ radio and television as part of their instructional system. Often, learners gain extra credits when they make use of the media. Sections of the printed correspondence course relate directly to TV and radio programmes, containing questions, and suggestions for further exercises. A useful function of TV or radio lies in the necessity of regularly spaced broadcasts. This has the virtue of compelling correspondence course students to keep to a regular schedule of study; the necessity of keeping pace with the broadcasts is an extra motivational factor in avoiding the high dropout rate among corresponding students. The TV programmes can deal directly with problems concerned with correspondence education. In Australia, the media have been used to provide some sense of communal identity to students taking correspondence courses by themselves, and who live miles apart.

The bulk of existing filmed courses in English language teaching do not follow any existing syllabus. This is clearly an impossibility when the aim is to sell the course as widely as possible, overriding a syllabus based upon national or local linguistic needs. It has been necessary to produce a separate syllabus on which the programmes can be based. The syllabus, therefore, reflects the particular virtues of film or television rather than the needs of the particular audience, or the requirements of a balanced ELT course. Thus, listening comprehension has dominated the course, since film is ideally suited to showing 'language in situations'. Further, the necessity of selling the series to a heterogeneous audience, and the impossibility of defining that audience in any way, has led to a preponderance of 'sugar' in relation to the teaching 'pill'. The bulk of the syllabus, therefore, tends to be confined to ancillary material. This is normally in the form of textbooks with, perhaps, additional material on tape or record. The onus is placed very heavily upon the unsupervised learner to get through a considerable amount of material between each transmission of the television series. The supplementary notes must inform the learner whether he is to cover the textbook and tape material before the programme, or whether the programme will introduce material which he must then follow up himself. The pacing of the course has to be carefully assessed. Assumptions have to be made about the study time available to the average viewer, and an estimate made of the amount of learning which is likely to take place in that time. The spacing of the television programmes has then to be arranged round that calculation. A usual fault in such filmed series is the compression of too much material into each weekly segment. If the lone learner cannot keep up a regular study schedule, he will remain behind the TV programmes, unless revision programmes are introduced every three or four weeks. Language learning is a long-term business, even for full-time students in supervised classes. For part-time, unsupervised students the process takes even longer, except for the fanatic few who are able to set aside all other responsibilities and devote a great deal of spare time to study. The syllabus for such students has to be graded and paced very gradually. The twenty-six-week course will achieve very little; broadcasting authorities have to be prepared for a commitment of two or three years. This is particularly true if the aim is a general English course which covers a number of different skills. A safer course of action, and one which allows a more efficient use of television, is to aim at a specific audience with a particular type of language skill. Simple conversational English for potential French tourists; reading skills for businessmen; speech practice for immigrants; note-taking and report-writing for secretaries and students: these types of courses restrict both audience and subject-matter. Profuse supplementary material will still be required, but the advantage lies in having an identified audience with specific needs, and therefore, greater motivation to learn. The disadvantage lies in convincing broadcasting authorities that they will gain more from teaching a specific audience and syllabus, than from attempting a general language course for an unidentified audience. When the course is aimed at an unsupervised learner, the more restricted its aim and potential audience, the more chance there is of organizing an integrated teaching system. When the aim is broad, and the audience unspecific, such integration is far more difficult to achieve.

Response: the Supervised Learner

The second stage of the link between studio and student takes place in the programme itself. This is the stage of student response, and involves making arrangements for the learner to participate in the programme. Some authorities argue that this is an undesirable element in televised instruction; that teachers should stay at the back of the classroom behind the students;

that students should not be allowed to take notes, or step out of their role as passive viewers. The television programme should have the learner's undivided attention throughout. Attention, however, is a major problem for any television producer. Any dramatic or informational presentation has to take account of varying attention on the part of the viewer from moment to moment. Every programme has to contain a certain amount of repetition; storylines cannot be too complex. Films of books are forced to present a simplified essence, simply because the film audience cannot hold too much information in mind at any one time. Educational programmes often attempt to retain attention by developing storylines which are exciting or amusing. This is especially true of language-teaching programmes. Surveys have been conducted on this very issue, and have found that there is no correlation between the entertainment and the educational value of a programme. Indeed, an interesting or amusing content can distract from the linguistic form, which is presumably the instructional point. The audience's attention span is always limited, but it is unlikely to be improved by variations in the programme tempo. The audience itself must be made to break out of its passive role, and to participate.

Secondly, a passive audience for an educational programme denies the importance of the reinforcement factor in learning. Experiment has shown that learning is greater when the classroom teacher can periodically go over the points covered in the television programme. Going off the air every five or ten minutes, to allow for the teacher to recapitulate, usually presents insuperable administrative problems, though it has been done. It also does not help the unsupervised learner. Reinforcement has to be built into the programme structure, and, clearly, reinforcement is more effective in language instruction if the student himself is asked to participate. Factors of attention and reinforcement are important in any educational television programme, but, in language teaching, they are side-effects of the third and most vital reason for encouraging audience response. Whichever language skill is being taught, the learner can only learn by using the material in some way. His participation may be speech, or writing something in his workbook; it may be passive participation, by mental selection of correct choices from a list. But he cannot be said to have learnt the skill unless he practises it through constant use.

If, therefore, an English language teaching programme simply consists of a dialogue storyline, designed to show the language being used in a particular situation, with all learner participation confined to post-programme activity, with teacher or textbook, then the effect of the programme will be minimal. There is little point in producing it at all. Such a format risks inattention, perhaps at the most crucial points, linguistically. There is no attempt to draw attention to, or to reinforce, the points being taught. And the programme merely demonstrates language, but does not teach it. The link between studio and student is only created by breaking up the programme, jumping from one activity to another, compelling student attention and encouraging his participation. In earlier sections we have discussed the necessity for an eclectic approach to language teaching; this discussion was based upon the nature of the language material itself. The same approach is now seen to be required because of the need to establish links between studio and student. It is of vital concern when we come to discuss programme format in the next section.

Many techniques for linking studio to supervised student have been mentioned in our inventory of language teaching skills. The supervisor can be trained to play a significant part in encouraging his students to respond to the television teacher; supplementary material can incorporate sections which the student must use during the programme itself. Such classroom techniques as choral drills, pattern drills with groups or individual students, the teaching of rhymes and songs can easily be conducted by the television teacher with the help and participation of the teacher. He can be asked, in the notes provided for his use, to bring certain objects to the classroom, or to provide certain simple pictures, which can then be incorporated into television drills. Students can be asked to manipulate these objects, to practise verb forms, prepositional phrases, and so on. The problem here is one of pacing and cueing. Experiment will show how long to allow for each exercise, and various forms of cueing devices can be tried to establish one which is acceptable and unambiguous. The teacher must be given full instructions on his part in this kind of response activity: he may have to select students for a particular question, hold up or point to objects himself, conduct his class during speech practice, draw or write things on the blackboard. The choice of exercise will depend upon the quality of the teacher available; such exercises are suitable where the teacher is not trained in language-teaching skills. More qualified teachers may resent the intrusion of television in such drill work which they regard as their own prerogative. Response, in this situation, may be confined to other language skills, more difficult for the classroom teacher to handle. A variety of language games and competitions can be incorporated into the programme, asking for student response. Clues might be presented on the screen for a crossword puzzle which is in the student's workbook, or which the teacher draws on the blackboard. A whole range of language activities involve selecting right from wrong answers or choosing correct answers from multiple choice lists. These activities involve response which might be verbal (saying the correct sentence, word, or number), or written (writing an answer down, or ticking one answer from several printed in the workbook). Examples of such exercises, in all skills, and at all levels of difficulty, have been given in earlier sections. Broader participation among supervised students can be encouraged by bringing students to the television studio, running language competitions and featuring the winners, or using certain schools or institutions in filmed or photographed activities relevant to a particular language point.

Response: the Non-supervised Learner

Response during the programme is more difficult to achieve with unsupervised students. There is far greater reticence when the lone learner is asked to respond out loud; nor is there any virtue in asking him to do so, when there is no supervisor to check his response. He may, however, produce a desired sound distinction sub-vocally, or he may record the television sound-track on tape, together with his own responses, for later comparison. The point of using speech exercises in a television programme is to free a teacher or supervisor to move around a student group and check responses. To incorporate such exercises in programmes for unsupervised learners achieves very little. A different technique is required. The emphasis will be less on practice drills, and more on test material. Thus, a home learner may be presented with sound contrasts which he may produce sub-vocally. The main teaching element is then a series of pictures which illustrate the relevant sound distinctions. The sound which accompanies each picture may be correct or incorrect, and the student's response depends on his ability to say which. This technique can be applied to all levels of the speech skill, and relies upon the assumption that the student's ability to recognize right from wrong spoken sounds and structures correlates with his ability to produce them. It is likely that sub-vocalization takes place in such exercises, but this is not an assumption which can be usefully depended upon for the purpose of programme construction. Similarly, the unsupervised learner cannot be asked to manipulate objects, or perform actions, to give a situational context to the language being taught. He is unlikely to perform such activities since he can imagine them quite satisfactorily. We are left with a variety of testing devices, suitable for the receptive skills of listening and reading. At the beginning stage, they encourage the learner to select correct from incorrect sounds and symbols; later he must make choices on the basis of his understanding of structure; and we can test his ability to understand what he hears and reads. In some television systems, it will be possible to arrange for viewers to send in written answers, or punched cards for central assessment. But elsewhere it will be necessary to provide self-correcting devices in the ancillary material which is sent to the unsupervised learner. This may be in the form of programmed books, or a list of answers at the back of the book. The learner may then be asked to write simple answers in his workbook, or to tick the correct answer, and he can look up the answers after the programme. Alternatively, answers may be given in the programme itself, or, with longer answers, they may be presented as part of the practice material in the subsequent programme.

Television quiz games admit the difficulty of involving the participation of the viewer when they provide the panel of participants themselves, and often inform the home viewers of the correct answers before the quiz panel begins. Although the unsupervised learner's motivation may be greater than that of the audience for entertainment programmes, we cannot assume that he has a viewing environment more conducive to learning. It is this factor which limits his participation in the learning process, during the programme itself, to observation and simple recognition procedures. And it is the same factor which has restricted the producers of ELT filmed series to the skills of listening and reading comprehension. The balance can be redressed by the use of carefully constructed ancillary notes and exercises, and by encouraging letters from viewers, and their participation in the programme. But, in general, the course constructor cannot rely upon the capability of the unsupervised learner to form a link with the studio during the programme itself.

Assessment: the Supervised Learner

The final stage of the link between studio and student is that of assessment. The problems here are less concerned with finding out the relevant information, than deciding exactly what it is we wish to know. There is a great deal of published research into various aspects of educational television, and much of it is relevant to any country and any audience at any level of development. The importance of the physical viewing conditions; the need for organized learning conditions, either by means of a supervisor or ancillary material; the technical problems of scriptwriting for television: these are everyday concerns of the television producer, they constitute part of his training, and they are open to experimental investigation. There is little need for further investigation into these variables for each type of programme in each country. One item of assessment which has consumed much time and effort in the past, has been the attempt to evaluate instruction by television against conventional instruction in the classroom.[3] From the point of view of pure learning, the results have often been inconclusive, and further lengthy investigations have attempted to assess the superiority of television with regard to student motivation and attitude. The difficulties of rating the effectiveness of television as a medium of instruction has made it impossible to advise educational planners on its effectiveness in relation to cost. In practice, of course, such assessments are rarely the basis for decisions on the establishment of educational television systems. Further experiments are, therefore, of somewhat academic interest. There is, however, little academic point in attempting to establish the superiority of television over other teaching means. Rarely will television be employed to the exclusion of other means of instruction, and, in a total teaching system, it is only one weapon in the armoury. It operates as part of a system, and it is therefore extremely difficult to examine the end result—the actual learning achieved—and then try to establish to which element in the system it can be attributed. The scale for grading television effectiveness cannot be the same for grading teacher effectiveness, or initial learner intelligence. It then becomes impossible to rate the grading scales against each other.

Subjective Reports

Two other types of assessment are frequently included in printed report sheets sent to teachers or to students. These attempt to assess the technical quality of a programme—whether sound or vision or both were defective in the viewer's particular case—and whether the programme content fitted in with his other learning activities—was the pace too rapid or too slow, the content too difficult or too easy. Information about these factors after the event can do no good at all, especially if the series is recorded days or weeks in advance of transmission. If the studio employs an off-air check, it is well aware of its own technical deficiencies; if the student's reception is poor for all transmissions, he knows to seek servicing advice. The assessment of such factors as pacing and level of difficulty is, again, a waste of time. If it is necessary, it is an indication that the first stage of the studio-student link has been omitted. There is little point in putting out an educational programme if these facts about the learner's syllabus are not known. The television programme, however brilliant, will have no effect if it is not closely integrated into the total teaching system, whether it be a supervised syllabus, or a textbook course. It may prove necessary to run pilot pragrammes for the purposes of assessing these factors; but this, too, constitutes part of the first stage of linking studio to student.

The only purpose in assessing educational television programmes is to establish how far they achieve what they set out
to do. There are a large number of elements in each such communication by television. Some of them can be dealt with in the
integration stage of the studio-student link. Some cannot be
handled at all—student attention, for example. But the construction of the television programme itself—the coding of the communication—depends upon a number of factors which may
need to be tested. A piece of information is sent from studio to
learner, and it may be presented in a number of ways. Which
particular method is selected will depend upon the ability and
experience of the writer and producer, and their knowledge of
other people's experience and experiments. This experience,
however, may relate to types of viewer-learners which differ to
some degree from the writer's immediate audience. Television
communication is a jumble of conventions. An audience may be
totally unaccustomed to cutting techniques, for example, which
may involve looking at the same picture from a different angle,
or from different distances. The conventions of animation may
be alien to the audience, or various design conventions. Unless
experiments have been conducted upon the particular audience
to discover acceptable and unacceptable conventions, it will be
necessary to run tests to find out whether they can be used in a
television presentation, and how far it is necessary to train the
audience in convention-recognition. In short, the writer-producer
needs to know, firstly, if the communication was successful, and
whether the student learnt what he was supposed to learn.
Second, if the results indicate a failure in the communication,
the writer-producer needs to be able to find out why it occurred,
and what he can do about it.

A method commonly employed to assess TV programmes is
the report card which asks students and teachers to send in their
subjective evaluation of the programme, under a number of
specified headings. The chance of learning anything useful from
this system is very small. What can be gained from knowing
whether the students found a programme very interesting/
interesting/not interesting? Or whether response to the television
teacher was good/fair/poor? An overwhelming number of
unfavourable replies may either indicate that the television

writer-producer is totally incompetent, or that the subject of the programme is universally detested. In discussing Lord Reith's saying: 'Few people know what they want and fewer still what they need', John Scupham notes: 'In relation to broadcasting it is a simple statement of facts familiar to every broadcasting man who has ever conducted a wide canvass of opinion in the search for new ideas and constructive suggestions.'[4] It is a laborious business to sort out the reasons for various attitudes expressed by students or teachers, and whether they are justified. It is equally laborious to try to decide what constitutes a statistical proportion significant enough to justify action. It may be that a teacher or student will note something which the television writer has over-looked—this depends upon the thoroughness of his preparation. But the main advantage of subjective evaluation sheets is the psychological effect they may have upon teachers and students. They may feel that they are being consulted and that their views are considered useful. And they are useful in building the link between student and studio. In language programmes, the viewer's evaluation may be in the form of letters to the television teacher, and they may as such be incorporated into the programme itself. They help to encourage the viewer's involvement with and participation in, the learning system. But as a means of assessing the real value of the programmes, they are of very little use. Some means of objective evaluation have to be sought, and this is more difficult to achieve with unsupervised learners than with viewers in organized classes.

Objective Evaluation

We are concerned, then, with the assessment of the communication which has taken place through a television programme. This is not the same as assessing the language ability of the student. Whether the TV programme slots into an existing syllabus, or whether it combines with ancillary notes to form its own teaching scheme, it is only part of the means whereby the student learns. In an achievement test it will only be possible to assign certain results to the effect of the television programme if it has handled one specific skill, or sub-skill. Even then, the interlocking of the

various language skills at every level will make it extremely difficult to make accurate assessments of the role of television. For
example, the role of TV may have been confined to letter or
word recognition skills. It is hardly possible, nor would it be
desirable, for students to avoid seeing letter and word forms
except on the television screen. The more integrated the means of
teaching, the better the course will be; and the more difficult it
will be to assess the effectiveness of any one element from the end
result. The only rough guide to the long-term effectiveness of
television in language teaching is to compare the achievement
test results of two groups over a period of time. Most previous
experiments have taken this form. One group uses television as part
of their instruction; a control group follows the same course without the addition of television. The number of variables in such
experiments are difficult to control. In some cultures and countries it will be difficult administratively to set up such groups;
parents whose children are deprived of television will not respond
to the plea that their children form part of an experiment. In
some areas it will be difficult to find a base test which will ensure
the compatibility of the two groups. Such variables as the intensity of exposure to television, and the relative quality of the two
teachers, may have an overwhelming influence upon the final
results.

Short-term effectiveness of some television programme has
been assessed by means of a simple test.[5] Five or six key points in
a programme are shaped into test questions; they may require
blank-filling, one-word answers, multiple-choice selection, or a
taped verbal response. Questions may be put on tape, or they
may be typed, each on a separate piece of paper. A sample of
viewing students are given these questions to answer just before
they see the television programme. Each student only answers
one question; where verbal replies are required, the teacher may
go round the class with a microphone, or separate students into
groups for individual recording. The total proportion of right
answers indicates the pre-programme ability of the student
sample on the key points. Immediately the programme is
finished, the same questions are given to the sample, though each
student will answer a different question from the one he answered
before the programme. The total proportion of right answers will

indicate the post-programme ability of the students on the key points. Comparison of the two sets of scores will indicate the success of the programme in communicating the key points.

Care needs to be taken with this type of test, as in all language testing. Test constructors need to be aware of the pitfalls of framing questions on language ability; they may wish to run pre-tests to eliminate weak questions; they have to be precise about what they are testing; and what skills are required from the student to produce an answer. Such a format can test sound differentiation, and letter and word recognition; it can test written and spoken structure. Meaning relationships can be tested, though contextual meaning cannot be tested, since the students will not have seen or heard the televised material before the programme. Where the supervisors themselves are asked to administer the test, they must be given full instructions and, preferably, practice, to ensure that they do not influence the results in any way. Where it is intended to test sound differentiation, for example, and the supervisors are not native English speakers, it may be necessary to present the test from the screen itself, at the very beginning and at the very end of the programme. Supervisors have to be clear about their exact role in these arrangements.

Such a testing scheme has two advantages: ease and speed of administration, and rapid assessment of results. The first advantage is of value to the hard-pressed teacher; the second advantage enables the television course writer to gain immediate feedback. If his programmes are not recorded too far in advance of transmission, it enables him to incorporate remedial action in later programmes, where necessary. He has to know how to interpret the results. If a particular question yields high scores in both tests, his programme has simply given extra practice, but taught nothing new. This tells him something about the integration of his programme with the total teaching scheme. If there is a significant increase in scores on a question, the programme has communicated the point successfully. If the two scores are low, or if high pre-programme scores decline, the programme has taught nothing about the tested item, and may have confused the students. Other factors than the programme presentation may be responsible for this: technical difficulties of reception, or in the viewing environment. The class may have been distracted for some minutes. The test supervisor will have to be provided with a test report form, so that such interference can be accommodated in the interpretation of the results. With due regard for all possible extraneous factors, the results may still indicate that the programme has not communicated the points satisfactorily. The problem then facing the television course writer is of finding out why. Where did the communication fail?

What went Wrong?

There are a number of methods available to the television course writer when he plans each teaching item in his programme. Which method he selects will depend upon his knowledge of his audience. Ideally, he should test his method before committing it to use in a programme. Otherwise, a failure in communication may be simply the result of bad preparation. A passage of printed material for reading practice may be rolled across the screen too rapidly for the average ability of the viewers; cueing devices may be ambiguous; the rhythm of a speech drill may be confusing; instructions to the viewing students as to how to respond to certain questions may be unclear; insufficient time might be allowed for response. Post-programme assessment might indicate communication failure over any one of these points, and it will be necessary to make careful observations and readjust accordingly. Failure might be due to faults in the technical structure of the programme. Important parts of a picture of a printed sentence may be lost in the cut-off area; an action may be demonstrated too quickly. There may be ambiguity between the information conveyed in the visual channel and the audio channel. Unless the two channels coincide to form a total piece of information, the viewer-listener will select one or the other channel, and may fail to understand the intended communication. A spoken commentary may have failed to draw the viewers' attention to the vital elements in a picture or printed sentence; a picture may not have illustrated precisely the point being made in the audio channel. Any one of these structural points may be the reason for a poor test result. In analysing the reasons for the result, it will be necessary to examine the method of presentation of the particular point once again, and decide whether the fault lies in the technical method of presentation. A good deal of experimental literature is available to guide the television producer and scriptwriter in his technical problems.

Controlled experiments have also looked into the conventions which are peculiar to television and other visual material which might be included in a television programme, such as film and still captions. A poor result in an assessment test may be attributable to the viewers' lack of familiarity with these conventions. Whereas experimental conclusions about the technical structure of television communication apply in all countries for all audiences, the same cannot be said of experiments in the conventions of the medium. Conventions have to be learned, and an audience becomes familiar with them only after prolonged exposure. For many years, film directors felt it necessary to begin with an establishing shot, and to link scenes in different locations by means of a shot series showing the protagonist leaving one building, getting into his car, driving his car, arriving at the next location and getting out of his car. It was felt that audiences could not make the conceptual leap from one location to the next without linking shots. The same problem beset the comic strip, and the conceptual jump between one picture and the next. Today, films frequently omit linking shots, and feel confident enough to delay establishing shots until some way into the plot. It is presumably felt that sophisticated audiences are sufficiently trained in the conventions of film to be able to make greater conceptual jumps. Television audiences today are familiar with the sight of TV cameras, microphone booms and other studio paraphernalia entering the shot in many types of television programme —a considerable departure from the strict conventions of a few years ago. Thus conventions change over a period of time, as audiences become accustomed to certain methods of communication and demand variety.

For less sophisticated audiences, it may be necessary to adopt conventions in television presentation which are outdated by modern standards. In terms of teaching effectiveness, there is no significant difference between the amount learned from a televised lecture and the same information conveyed in a more interesting format. A producer understandably wishes to make interesting programmes, but, in so doing, he may be using conventions unfamiliar to his audience. An object may be shown in long shot, and then close-up, from the front or from the side. Some audiences may be confused by such changes in angles. Cutting between shots, from interiors to exteriors, or from one person to another in a conversation, depends upon assumptions which the audience may not hold. We assume that two people are conversing, though we may know, intellectually, that the filmed shots may have been taken days apart, each person speaking to no one. We accept a convention which some types of audience may not. Similarly, the sudden appearance of superimpositions, or the mixing of one picture into another may cause problems in some countries. An experiment conducted in Ethiopia indicated that some children there were unable to follow a story told in sequential strip form; they did not relate the pictures to each other at all, but discussed each picture as a separate entity. The same perceptual block may occur when they are faced with cuts and mixes in a television programme. It may be necessary to set up an experiment with a sample group of the potential audience for a series, and find out which conventions are acceptable and which are not. It may then be necessary to employ less intricate conventions, and attempt to train the viewers towards a more sophisticated acceptance of television presentation techniques. For example, early programmes may have to be presented almost totally in long shots and panning movements, the teacher in the studio moving from demonstration objects to blackboard, or overhead projector. The students then follow his movements as they would follow their classroom teacher. Gradually, they may be trained to accept cuts by such introductory phrases as 'Let's look at this more closely', or 'Now I'm going to show you a film.' Eventually such phrases will become redundant, and the conventions will be established. There is no way of knowing which conventions are acceptable for a particular audience without specific experiment, geared to the audience's cultural and linguistic background.

Pictures of all types feature prominently in language-teaching television programmes, and, again, they may be based upon assumptions about acceptable design conventions which do not always hold true. Limited film or studio facilities may make it impossible to demonstrate actions properly, and still photographs or drawings may have to be used. A photograph of someone running may be meaningless to an audience unaccustomed to seeing frozen action, and unable to make assumptions about the photographic convention. Three-dimensional perspective may cause perceptual difficulties for some students. Certain design conventions are used frequently in textbooks: lines behind a running figure, or a car, to indicate speed; speech or thought balloons; symbols incorporated to indicate puzzlement (question mark), or shock (exclamation mark). Sequential stories told in still pictures have already been mentioned as a possible area of confusion. Film animation techniques can also be confusing, since they are so unrealistic. We accept jerky movements, and impossible contortions of the body in animated cartoons, just as we accept the inhuman voices and rapid-fire music which accompany them. We cannot suddenly switch over to real-life situations and normal speaking voices, for listening comprehension purposes; the mixture of conventions would be absurd and confusing. Again, experiments must be set up for each new audience, to establish which conventions are already available, and which have to be taught. Such experiments have wider implications than the assessment of a television programme. Visual perception plays an important part in all aspects of language teaching and education in general. Television programmes provide the scope for a wide range of graphic material which can train students to perceive and understand further visual material outside their language course of study. Photographs of events, aerial photographs, microscopic blow-ups can be analysed for information; graphs and charts can be incorporated for comprehension work, or structure formation; diagrams of science experiments, or street plans; cartoons in various styles from pin-men to naturalistic paintings, with or without captions; posters and advertisements of various kinds, from commercial products to health campaigns; cutaways of landscapes such as frequently appear in geography textbooks. These and many other types of visual material may require special attention for the unsophisticated student, and, since language teaching by television relies heavily upon the visual element, there is every reason to incorporate training in visual perception in the programmes.

Finally, a programme assessment may indicate poor communication over an entire method of presentation. A chemistry experiment can be shown in a number of ways: a teacher may illustrate it by means of a diagram on a blackboard or a caption; a teacher may actually conduct the experiment in front of the camera; or an animated film might be used to indicate the chemical changes taking place. A programme may wish to teach a concept such as counting; which method would show this most clearly? We may make a location film in a bazaar; we may actually count objects in the studio; we may simply present still captions while a voice counts the objects shown in each picture. A language programme may be dealing with the intonation pattern of questions in English: is it enough to show a teacher saying the sentence, perhaps indicating the rising tone with a gesture? Should we superimpose some graphic device as he says the sentence? Should we write out the sentence and indicate the rising tone with a drawn line, or with a finger? These alternatives are of more than academic interest. Cost is often a deciding factor in such matters, but when we choose still drawings over an expensively shot film, we have to know how much we are sacrificing in terms of the communication. Again, experimentation in this area is not necessarily universally applicable. Some cultures react differently to different methods of presentation, since each method is not of equal familiarity. A particular item can be presented in three or four different ways, and presented to three or four compatible groups, which form a sample of the viewing audience. A test of these groups will indicate whether there is any significant difference in the teaching effectiveness of the various methods. The cost of each can then be weighed against their educational efficiency.

Assessment: the Non-supervised Learner

Discussion so far has centred upon programmes aimed at supervised learners, since assessment is obviously easier in an organized educational environment. Subjective assessment of unsupervised learners can be obtained from door-to-door visiting, postal questionnaires, and viewers' panels of various kinds. The only way of objectively assessing the effectiveness of the programme as a teaching instrument is temporarily to form unsupervised learners into organized learning groups.[6] Long-term assessment can be carried out by periodic examinations held at local centres; these at least will show how the unsupervised learners are faring in their language ability. They will not show the part which the television programmes have played in the final result, and how much is due to the student's own unsupervised efforts. The simple test described earlier can be given to a sample group of viewers, who are brought together for a particular programme, and tested before and after the transmission. The administrative and financial problems of arranging such group viewing and testing are extremely complex in most countries, but it is the only way of making an immediate and useful assessment of how far the programme communicates what it sets out to communicate. It may be possible to organize such groups on a regular basis, taking different localities and different samples in turn. Such a scheme provides a regular system of feedback to the television course writer. It also enables him to run other tests to establish where communication has broken down. If it proves impossible to organize unsupervised learners, there is no way of assessing the value of the programmes, and the link between studio and learner remains incomplete.

Notes

1. Chu and Schramm: op. cit. 1967, pp. 13–15
2. Renée F. Erdos: *Teaching by Correspondence* Longmans/UNESCO 1967
3. See Helen Coppen (1968); Chu and Schramm (1967): *Research in Instructional Television and Film* U.S. Office of Education 1967
4. Scupham: op. cit. 1967, p. 40
5. John Gartley and Richard Sherrington: 'Evaluation and Testing in ETV in Ethiopia' *E.T.I.* Vol. 3 No. 2 1969
6. J. M. Trenaman: *Communication and Comprehension* Longmans 1967

10 The Programme Format

Recapitulation: The Total System

We come, finally, to the problem of format. How is all the material in the inventory of language-teaching functions to be sifted and a selection made? How is the selection we make to be related to the many elements in the communication between studio and student, so that we end up with a finished programme? There are so many factors to be considered that any examples we present can only be of use to educational planners in certain countries and educational systems. We can, however, begin with a basic premise common to them all: they all wish to teach English. From this premise, it will be useful to summarize the decisions which all planners will have to make with regard to their particular situation. Upon this analysis rests the final decision about the type of programme they wish to present, in order to teach English by television, and the type of format which should be employed.

There are, firstly, the *administrative* factors:

(a) the level of national development; the political, economic and social influences upon the character of the educational system; the implications of introducing technology into the system.

(b) budgetary provision for education, and the proportions to be allocated to the various elements in the system.

(c) the availability and quality of the media: textbooks, classroom supplies, technological hardware and software.

(d) the existence and quality of an administration; the degree of control of the administration over the educational system, and other implicated organizations—the postal system, the broadcasting system.

(e) the existence and quality of a teaching body; whether

teachers can be found and trained, or whether learners should be regarded as unsupervised.

(f) the facilities for smooth communication between members of the teaching team—supervisor, broadcaster, administrator, learner so that each knows who does what.

Secondly, there are the *pedagogical* factors:

(a) the existence and type of curriculum; the subject balance it maintains, and the degree of integration of subjects; the relationship of the curriculum to national examinations, or other diplomas or qualifications which might be awarded.

(b) The existence and type of a syllabus for English-language instruction; the reasons for including English in the curriculum; the extent to which the syllabus reflects these reasons.

(c) the age and mother-tongue of the learners; their motivation for learning; the identification of specific points in their programme of study which may require emphasis—first year of secondary education, the pre-university year; the introduction of new methods and textbooks at certain points.

(d) the selection of items from the inventory of language skills, and their disposal among the media available.

Assuming that the analysis so far leads the educational planner to contemplate the use of television to teach English, there are, lastly, the *technical* factors to be considered:

(a) the amount of airtime available; the convenience of available time-slots for the target audience.

(b) the technical facilities of the studio; if recording facilities are available, the balance to be maintained between repeat transmissions of a few programmes, and single transmissions of many different programmes.

(c) the conditions at the receiving end; classroom size or typical domestic viewing conditions; receiver servicing facilities.

(d) the sophistication of the audience with regard to television conventions, and different types of visual material.

At first sight, such a factor analysis seems to set out an increasingly severe series of limitations upon the planner's freedom of action. As the choices become narrower, according to his own situation, we seem to be admitting the necessity for a microstructural approach to teaching—a certain type of English for a certain type of student in a certain type of situation. Are we, then, back to the initial problem, with which this book began, of matching highly specific educational criteria with the economics of the mass media?

In fact the factors we have listed do not form a sequential pattern of decisions, each one specifying the limitations of action more narrowly than the last. These factors are, in practice, interdependent, together forming a description of any system of education, depending upon the answers which each situation provides. The educational planner who has to juggle with them has an unenviable task. The most dynamic political will and the most efficient administration can do nothing if the teaching manpower is simply not available. The absence of convenient airtime will involve a reordering of the teaching system, perhaps placing an undesirable burden upon the teacher or the textbook course. The absence of an organized syllabus may render the TV programmes totally ineffective. A TV series tightly integrated into a classroom teaching system is nonetheless useless if the administration cannot keep the studio in communication with the classroom. Each planner's analysis will differ; but the overriding criterion will remain the same—each system has to be as integrated as possible. The more integrated the system, the more efficient it is: it both teaches efficiently and the cost ratios between the various elements are correctly in proportion to their importance. Where the system is not integrated, each element attempts to do more than it can efficiently handle, costs escalate, standards decline, and the planner has failed in his job.

The Role of Television

Each analysis will differ and each approach to the problem of integration will differ. Hence, each choice of a television programme format will differ. ELT programmes produced for television throughout the world in the last few years have generally set their sights low, and concentrated on limited teaching aims. The choice of a restricted aim often produces a very successful programme format. A whole series might be designed to teach writing skills. A very entertaining series can be built around the problem of teaching meaning relationships. Several filmed series have been based upon amusing or exciting storylines, aimed at the practice of listening comprehension. Children's television programme formats are ideal for such activities as pre-reading games, object naming, the introduction of various design conventions. These types of programme are successful television in that they entertain and hold the attention through the medium of the target language. They may be successful in teaching the limited range of items which each attempts. But they are only part of the language-teaching process. To be really successful, they must have been designed to fit into a total teaching process, in which the bulk of language teaching is carried on somewhere else in the system—by the classroom teacher, textbook, tapes, records, or any combination of these elements.

Another type of format, also with a restricted aim, might be employed to practise language items which are introduced elsewhere in the system. The major problem for television here is the availability of airtime, which can rarely provide the intensity of practice which is required for most language skills. The practice might consist of thirty minutes of picture-word matching, reading comprehension, speed reading exercises, speech drills, sound differentiation practice. Thirty minutes, however, is a long period of time over which to retain viewers' attention, however well motivated, however well supported by the efforts of a classroom teacher. Ultimately, it is boring television. It may be necessary, in such an arrangement, to slot in 'rest pauses' into the programme format, to break the monotony—an exciting film might be shown, an activity might be introduced using the learners' mother-tongue, the television might go blank for a few minutes to allow time for the teacher to carry out classroom activity, or for the home learner to write in his notebook. Practice drills in the classroom are less boring, simply because the teacher can pace the lesson according to the feeling of the class. The pace of a television programme is fixed. The more concentrated its material, the more built-in redundancy the programme requires to retain attention. Such redundancy may be in the form of irrelevant material, or activity on the part of the viewer. It may be simply in the form of repetition of key sequences in the programme.

Alternatively, the programme format can be given a variety which will not only retain the viewers' interest and attention, but will also continue to provide meaningful language activity throughout. In any particular teaching system, specific roles may be allotted to the television programme, as to the other elements in the process. This does not mean that the television programme cannot also provide teaching information or practice activities which are, strictly speaking, allotted to other elements in the system for in-depth coverage. Factors of viewer concentration and attention suggest that TV should do this. The only condition for the infringement of the boundaries of the teaching system in this way is that the teacher and the student should be fully informed of what the programme is doing.

In short, we are suggesting an eclectic approach to the problem of format for a language-teaching programme by television. The planner will give specific language-teaching aims to the programme producer. In addition, the producer will be free to add further language activities to his programmes, as supplementary material for the intensive teaching of these activities, handled elsewhere in the system. The producer can then put together a balanced programme: balanced externally, in relation to the other elements in the total teaching system; balanced internally, in that the programme will teach something, give practice in something, be interesting enough to retain viewer attention for its duration, and combine all these elements into a homogeneous whole. Such a format contains the flexibility which the classroom teacher possesses. It allows for a balance between concentrated activities and mechanical activities; between the viewers' passive attention and his active participation. It also allows for the insertion of remedial action when necessary. The kind of testing referred to in the previous section may reveal that one particular point has not been successfully communicated in a programme. A later programme can then be arranged to contain a slot which goes over this material again. This type of flexible format will vary from country to country, from situation to situation, from programme to programme. The successful writer/producer will be able to juggle with the many elements in such a format, and still be able to provide a programme which hangs together as a single unit.

Programme Theme

Some kind of theme is needed; a peg on which to hang the various language activities we wish to teach and practise. A major difficulty here is the artificiality of the teaching process. To show language in natural situations in which it is used is clearly not enough: apart from dealing with only one type of language skill (and at an advanced stage at that) such a procedure attempts to ignore the conventions of language learning, with which every learner is familiar. Until he is familiar with the material, a learner needs constant repetition; he needs to have the foreign-language material, spoken or written, presented to him at a moderate pace which enables him to grasp it; he needs to understand what he is doing and what he is working towards. These features of language learning are as true of the classroom student as of the lone learner with his textbook, and the learner in front of a TV screen. They all point to the artificiality of the learning process. To ignore this fact is to ignore the legitimate demands of the learner and considerably reduce the effectiveness of the programme.

Nonetheless, a large number of ELT programmes on television throughout the world have built a format upon language spoken naturally in 'real' situations. Such a format may be a domestic situation, set in England or America, or in the particular learner's own environment. The latter course of action only makes sense where English is a second language, and where the learner's understanding of 'natural' spoken or written English can be reinforced by everyday contact. It is the technique for teaching immigrants to English-speaking countries, and may be of use in certain parts of Africa and India. Extensions of this approach might present language in exciting or amusing stories in serial form. Literature can be plundered for an abundant store of material—not only the usual repertoire of stories from English or American literature, but also the literature of the learner's own culture, written originally either in English or the mother-tongue. Depending upon the available studio facilities and budget, these storylines can be developed in studio action, on film, or in drawings and still photographs.

The problem with this approach is the bridge which needs to

be built between, on the one hand, the easy flow of the storyline and the language style such a flow requires, and, on the other hand, the artificiality of the teaching demands of the programme. If the object is listening comprehension, or spoken drills, the story will have to be broken up at intervals with teaching segments. These intervals will have to be fairly closely spaced, if the learner is required to remember pieces of the story. However, the more broken-up the storyline becomes, the more difficult it is to follow the flow of the narrative. Constant repetition and recapitulation is required, and this constitutes redundant airtime. The range of language activities which can be easily incorporated in such a literary format is also strictly limited. If the format wishes to include reading or writing practice, the story has to be put into its literary context, perhaps introducing the author. In a domestic format, the protagonist has to be made into a journalist, or a letter-writer, so that the writing activity fits into the 'naturalness' of the format.

The main difficulty lies in the 'single concept' approach to a twenty- or thirty-minute television programme. This requires a considerable degree of attention on the part of the viewer, even in a straight documentary film or dramatic presentation. If he is also expected to distance himself from the storyline every so often—to observe, learn and practise the form of language beneath the content—then either form or the content, or both, will suffer. Either the learner will be so interested by the storyline that he will regard the teaching segments as distractions; or he will concentrate so much on the teaching segments that the storyline ceases to be important. A serial storyline, developed over thirteen or twenty-six episodes, implies that the theme—the peg—is more essential than the language which the programmes are supposedly teaching. A series of individually complete programmes has only one advantage—that a different type of language skill can be introduced in each programme.

The implication seems to be that the programme format should not be so engrossing that it distracts from the main purpose of the programmes—teaching language. This, of course, is the problem which faces the commercially filmed series, which assumes that the sugar on the pill has to be sweet enough to make people watch the programme in the first place. In practice, such series do themselves a disservice, in that sugar and pill are competing with each other for the viewers' attention, and the ultimate result is bound to be dissatisfying.

Twenty or thirty minutes is too long a period over which to expect viewers to maintain interest and concentration. The solution is not to make the theme less interesting or amusing in case it should distract; it is rather to reduce the length of time in which the student is asked to concentrate. A thirty-minute programme can be broken up into five or six sections, each requiring different forms of student attention. Incorporated into these sections, or slotted between them, the teaching sections can appear as simply part of the overall programme format, and not as separate entities which involve a mental conversion from content to form, from theme to language. The various segments of such a 'magazine' format can be connected together in theme either tightly or loosely, depending on the age and type of audience, and the particular uses to which the learners will put their language ability. A series for young children might be simply a ragbag of unconnected games, stories, films and pictures. One programme might be loosely built around a theme, such as 'animals', 'toys', 'towns', and so on. At a more advanced level, programmes might be constructed around more adult themes. For the home learner, they might be such topics as newspapers, sports, travel. In some countries, home learners might benefit from more specific topics, such as elementary hygiene, or malaria eradication, or erosion. English-language programmes on these subjects do not aim to teach the subjects themselves; ideally, they are being dealt with elsewhere in the education system. They provide additional material, or reinforcement, for existing instruction. In certain countries, there may be a direct relevance of English instruction to these subjects: public health posters and leaflets may be in English; instruction manuals for farm equipment may only be available in English. Elsewhere, such instruction will be carried out in the mother-tongue, and the English course may be part of quite different educational objectives. There is still no reason why the themes employed should not relate to, and help to reinforce, the mother-tongue instruction. They may take a broader approach than the conventional instruction, or concentrate on one element in the course. As far as possible, the programmes should be written in collaboration with the authorities responsible for the subject being dealt with, so that each knows what the other is doing in the total teaching scheme.

The subject of malaria, for example, can be broken down into a number of sections: statistics for the country or the continent; cause of the disease; symptoms of the disease; available cures; plan of campaign for malaria eradication; precautions that can be taken. None of these elements need be dealt with exhaustively. Each can be presented in a number of ways, depending upon the language skills being practised. Pictures, charts, maps, diagrams; interviews, demonstrations, acted sequences; newspaper reports, posters, leaflets—the art lies in presenting the sections in different ways so as to vary the type of activity required from the learner. The format has flexibility, in that any one section may be given emphasis, either because of the language skill it practises, or because the malaria eradication authorities feel that it should be given prominence. The approach can be either broad or specific; in either case, the format needs to have variety in theme, presentation and pacing.

Sample Formats

As examples, we can discuss three types of programme format. This is a dangerous procedure, in that they will only refer to certain types of teaching situation, and the reader may not recognize them as being comparable to his own. However, the examples will help to illustrate the approach we have taken to format: a single theme, broken up to allow for a variety of language skills, for the need to keep the viewers' attention, and for fluctuations in concentration. A large number of programme formats can be devised which vary from these examples. But the variations will only be a question of balance. Certain language skills might be given more weight than they are in the examples; the relation of language skill to theme, employed in the examples, might be written in a number of different ways. Whatever the variations, whatever the balance created, the value of such an eclectic approach remains the same.

The examples are set out in the form of programme plans. No attempt is made to script them precisely, since each situation will vary with regard to such problems as the nationality of the presenter, the use of English and mother-tongue, the 'tone' of the script (formal or informal). Studio and production facilities will also vary, and suggestions are made on a number of presentation techniques in each section.

FORMAT ONE
SITUATION

(a) This is a first-year English course, aimed at young children who view in schools, supervised by teachers who are not native-speakers of English, and who are not highly trained.

(b) English is the national second language, and a full range of language skills has to be acquired.

(c) Television time is available only once a week. It is decided that the TV programmes should introduce, or teach, each segment of a graded English course. The teacher, with the help of a textbook course, will provide the bulk of the practice material required during the classroom lessons.

(d) In the first year of the course, the main emphasis is upon the recognition and production of the sounds and spellings of English (phonological and graphological realization); the recognition and production of spoken structures; the understanding of the meanings of simple items in the students' environment, though no systematic teaching of meaning is attempted.

SETTING

Simple studio setting, attractive designs which appeal to young children. Playroom/workroom atmosphere. Minimum abrupt cutting; presenters to move openly from one activity to another within the room. Two presenters. Live animals—a cat on a table, a dog on a stool, a bird on a stick in a cage.

PROGRAMME PLAN

1. *Listening.* Presenter introduces animals, using structure and words taught in previous programmes and practised by teacher in the classroom.

The cat		sitting		stool
The dog	is	sitting standing	on the	table
The bird		standing		stick

Presenter 2 enters shot, and asks questions, which Presenter 1 answers.

the cat		sitting		stool?	
Is the dog		sitting standing	on the	table?	Yes/No
the bird		standing		stick?	

2. *Listening and Repeating.* Presenter 1 moves to new area. Explains present continuous question form, in vernacular, and demonstrates its Tune 2 intonation. This may be reproduced on a clarinet, after the production of each example. The clarinet is probably best not seen. The Presenter must emphasize the *sound* of the structure. He asks the viewers to repeat each sentence after him; he cues them by beating time and whispering each response. After each response the clarinet repeats the tune.

3. *Pre-reading.* Presenter 2 shows a series of pictures. Each picture contains two sets of shapes: 3 dogs/3 cats in silhouette; 2 cats/4 birds; 3 squares/4 rectangles; 2 'F' shapes/3 'E' shapes, and so on. The viewers are asked to differentiate the shapes, either naming them in English or the vernacular, or replying yes or no to the Presenter's questions.

4. *Listening*

(a) A film shows Presenter 1 walking, followed by dog walking, followed by cat walking. The dog looks round at cat, the Presenter looks round at dog. The cat starts running, the dog starts running, the Presenter starts running. Presenter 2 gives commentary, introducing structure:

$$\left.\begin{array}{l} \text{The cat} \\ \text{The dog} \\ \text{He} \end{array}\right\} \text{ is } \left\{\begin{array}{l} \text{walking} \\ \text{running} \end{array}\right.$$

(b) Studio. Presenter 2 demonstrates walking, running; explains the meaning. Demonstrates walking/running round the table, round the stool, round the chair, and so on.

(c) Film. The cat is running round a tree. Followed by the dog. Followed by Presenter 1. They all run round a house. Presenter 1 puts a lead on the dog. The cat, the dog and the Presenter walk back, round the house, and round the tree. Presenter 2 provides the commentary:

$$\left.\begin{array}{l} \text{He} \\ \text{The dog} \\ \text{The cat} \end{array}\right\} \text{ is } \left\{\begin{array}{l} \text{running} \\ \text{walking} \end{array}\right\} \text{ round the } \left\{\begin{array}{l} \text{tree} \\ \text{house} \end{array}\right.$$

5. *Speaking.* Present a series of still pictures which illustrate examples from the following table. Presenter 1 asks the questions, Presenter 2 gives the answers:

$$\text{Is } \left\{\begin{array}{l} \text{the cat} \\ \text{the dog} \end{array}\right\} \begin{array}{|c} \left\{\begin{array}{l} \text{sitting} \\ \text{standing} \end{array}\right\} \text{ on } \left\{\begin{array}{l} \text{the table?} \\ \text{the stool?} \end{array}\right. \\ \hline \left\{\begin{array}{l} \text{running} \\ \text{walking} \end{array}\right\} \text{ round } \left\{\begin{array}{l} \text{the tree?} \\ \text{the house?} \end{array}\right. \end{array} \text{ Yes/No}$$

After sufficient examples, ask the teacher to divide the class into two parts; one to ask questions, one to give the answers.
The question sequence may take one of the following forms, or combine two or three forms:

Picture:	a cat *sitting* on a table
Presenter:	CUE '*standing* on the table?'
Class Q:	'Is the cat *standing* on the table?'
Class A:	'No'

OR:
Picture:	a cat sitting on a *table*
Presenter:	CUE 'sitting on a *stool*'
Class Q:	'Is the cat sitting on a *stool*?'
Class A:	'No'

OR: *Picture:*   a cat *sitting* on a *table*
          Presenter: CUE '*running* round a *tree*'
          Class Q: 'Is the cat *running* round a *tree*?'
          Class A: 'No'

'Yes' and 'No' answers to be included. Full instructions with examples to be given in the vernacular. Teacher to be informed of drilling procedure in ancillary notes for explanation to class before the programme.

6. *Reading.* Presenter 1 shows picture of cat standing on a table. The word 'stand' is written on the picture. Animate out '-and'. Mix to caption with /st/ in bottom half, and st/sk/sl/sh in top half. Ask viewers to find the matching shape: st/st.
—Repeat with picture and the word 'stool'. Explain the meaning of the word; animate out '-ool'. Mix to caption showing /st/ with sl/sh/sk/st.
—Repeat process with 'stick'.

7. *Listening.* Presenter 2 introduces the following story, which is told on film, animation, still photographs or drawings:

A bird is standing on a stool (under a tree in the picture)
A cat is looking at the bird
The bird is running round the tree
The cat is running round the tree
The bird is sitting on the tree (branch? stick?)

         *   *   *

The cat is standing on the stool
A dog is looking at the cat
The cat is running round the tree
The dog is running round the tree
The cat and the bird are sitting on the tree (or two sentences in the singular)

         *   *   *

The dog is standing on the stool
A man is looking at the dog (he has a gun in the picture)
The dog is running round the tree
The man is running round the tree
The dog and the cat and the bird are sitting on the tree (or three sentences in the singular)

*   *   *

The man is cutting down the tree (explain in vernacular if necessary)
(Animate the dog and cat into the man's sack)
The man is walking to the house
(Tilt up to roof of house)
Here is the bird. The bird is sitting on the house

*   *   *

(This story may be repeated by Presenter 2, *this time speaking direct to the camera*. At certain points, still pictures from the story may be used as a stimulus for specific questions for the viewers to answer, with 'Yes' or 'No'.)

8. *Speaking*

(a) Presenter 1 introduces a series of pictures, and says a word to identify each one:

*st*ool	*st*and	*st*ick
*sch*ool	*sk*ip	*sk*ate
*sp*ot	*sp*ill	*sp*ell

(The initial /st/sk/sp/ sounds cause difficulties for speakers of the audience's mother-tongue.)

(b) Close-up of Presenter's face. He says each word for the viewers to repeat after him.

(c) The pictures are shown in a different sequence for the viewers to identify. Teachers are asked to check their students' pronunciation of the initial consonants.

9. *Writing.* Presenter 2 is seen writing (overshoulder or mirror shot). He writes/stick/story/stand/stool/ and, as he does so, recapitulates the sections of the programme in which these words occurred, using the vernacular. He then writes the /st/ shape a number of times, and suggests that the viewers practise writing this for themselves in the spaces provided in their notebooks.

10. End the programme.

COMMENTS

This programme plan is extremely simple, and yet provides a good deal of language practice, covering a number of activities. Each section may be longer or shorter, depending upon airtime available, and the amount of material it is necessary to cover in a programme. To allow one particular section to run on too long risks loss of concentration on the part of the viewers. After a few minutes, their attention needs to be drawn to a new idea, involving a different type of activity, yet related to the main language-teaching purpose of the programme. Thus, they can relax and enjoy the presentation of Section 4, before having to concentrate upon the organization of a group drill in Section 5. Each section is thus planned to contrast with the sections before and after it in terms of the type of participation required of the viewer.

For young children, it may be necessary to break up such a format even further by the introduction of more 'redundant' material—games, songs, amusing film sequences. It may also be necessary to link each section by showing a wide shot of the studio with both presenters and their relative position. This will depend upon the conventions available to the children, and what they are prepared to accept. Thus, Sections 7 and 8 may have to be linked by Presenter 2, who closes his story book, and walks across to Presenter 1 who is looking at some pictures. Later, such links may be dispensed with.

FORMAT TWO
SITUATION

(a) This is a third- or fourth-year English course, aimed at a predominantly adult audience which views at home, unsupervised.

(b) English is regarded as a foreign language; students are exposed to English language newspapers, magazines, products, radio broadcasts. A full range of language skills is to be acquired.

(c) TV time is available once a week. Students are used to watching TV in their mother-tongue, and a full range of TV conventions is available to them.

(d) Students have a textbook which is linked to the TV programmes, and the language teaching data must be allocated between these two media. Television is the only means of giving students practice in listening and speaking, though the range of structural and lexical material is too great to be handled by TV, and is introduced in the textbook before the student watches the programme. Conversely, the TV programmes are given the task of providing stimulus for reading and writing practice which is organized in the textbook.

(e) The theme selected is 'Problems caused by Traffic in Towns'. The structure used in this programme plan is comparative patterns.

SETTING

One presentation area is required, and an acting area which represents the office of a town planner. The programme plan assumes facilities for shooting sound film, animation techniques, and presenting a full range of caption material.

PROGRAMME PLAN

1. *Listening*

(a) The Presenter is interviewing people in the street. Some are interviewed face on; some interviews take place as commentary to film of road congestions, lorries unloading in busy roads, pedestrians unable to move about easily, and so on. The interviewer is shown to be taking notes of the interviews. All interviews are scripted, and contain the following comparative forms:

(1) wider/narrower/safer . . . than . . .
(2) more dangerous/more crowded/more beautiful . . . than . . .
(3) Some lorries are *bigger* than the buses
(4) The lorries are *noisier* than the cars
(5) The shopping centre is *busier* than the industrial area
(6) On Sundays the streets are *prettier* than on Mondays
(7) The housewives are *angrier* than the office workers
(8) This street is ugly, but the traffic makes it *uglier*
(It is assumed that these comparative forms have already been introduced to the student in his textbook.)

(b) The Presenter in the studio, with his notebook. He introduces the theme of the programme, and begins to refer to his notes. He picks out sentences, for which split pictures are shown:
Which street is wider/narrower/safer?
Which road is more dangerous/more crowded/more beautiful?
(Each half of each picture may be lettered or numbered. Viewers must say the letter or number of the correct picture.)

2. *Reading*

(a) Presenter says: 'Some lorries are *bigger* than buses.'
Picture: a bus (in ½ screen) 'This bus is big.'
a lorry (in ½ screen) 'This lorry is bigger.'
(The word 'big' is shown; it is enlarged to 'bigger', and the doubled consonant visually emphasized and explained by the Presenter.)
Repeat with:
'Spain is hot. Brazil is *hotter* than Spain.'
'Dad is fat. Mum is *fatter* than Dad.'

(b) Continue this procedure to show how the /y/ in 'noisy/busy/pretty/angry/ugly' changes to /i/ in the comparative form. Use the sentences from the interviews, and still pictures from the interview film.

3. *Writing.* Refer the viewer to his textbook, where a list of comparative patterns is set out. In each case, the doubled consonant, or the /i/ has been omitted. Show five or six pictures from the previous reading exercise, in jumbled order. Give the viewer enough time to find the correct sentence in his textbook, and fill in the doubled consonant or /i/.

4. *Listening.* Studio scene. Presenter with his notebook talks to a town planner about traffic problems. The planner moves about his office, referring to charts, diagrams, scale models of streets, and other visual material. He explains how some towns develop in the centre, beyond the capacity of feeder roads; how other towns have excellent feeder roads which draw in the traffic which cannot then be accommodated in the centre. Both must be planned together. He shows how towns can be divided into areas, residential, shopping, commercial, industrial.

Write in sentences from the following tables:

	houses			
There are	more shops	in (area)	A	than in B
	fewer offices		C	D
	factories			

	room			
	space	A	B
There is more less	traffic	in (area) than in
	movement	C	D
	smoke		

5. *Speaking.* Presenter shows sentences from his notes:
    e.g. There are more factories in A than in B.
Viewer must transform sentence, using 'fewer':
    e.g. There are fewer factories in B than in A.
Repeat with an example using 'less'. Explain the different usage, if not already covered in the textbook. Present a number of jumbled examples for the viewer to transform verbally. This practice may be extended beyond the confines of the immediate context, and pattern, thus:

There is more oil in Iran than in France
OR: More oil is produced in Iran than in France
OR: Iran produces more oil than France

6. *Listening.* Back to the town planner in his office. He refers to large statistical charts to demonstrate the following:

Car manufacturer's figures:

They bought more
petrol
oil
steel
paint
in 1971 than in 1968

Hospital figures:

There were more
deaths
injuries
accidents
casualties
in 1971 than in 1968

7. *Speaking.* Sentences from the listening section are displayed. The viewers are asked to make the correct transformations:

They bought more steel in 1971 than in 1968
They bought —— steel in 1968 than in 1971
There were more accidents in 1971 than in 1968
There were —— accidents in 1968 than in 1971

Notes:

(a) The viewers' response is to be verbal; the stimulus and the correct answer may be presented verbally by the Presenter or written out on captions and animated.

(b) If passive constructions have been taught, the comparative patterns may be rearranged:
More oil was produced . . .
Fewer deaths were caused . . .

8. *Listening.* A film of a traffic accident between a lorry driver and a cyclist. The bicycle is damaged. Both begin to argue. A policeman appears, and listens to both stories while taking down notes in his book.

All scripted, using all the comparative patterns practised in the programme so far.

The policeman goes off to write his report.

9. *Reading*. A set of street signs flashed on the screen for rapid
   recognition by the viewers. After each sign, the meaning of
   each is shown briefly: Stop, Danger, Turn Left, No Entry,
   No Parking, Crossing, etc.

10. *Speaking*. The Presenter introduces words used by the lorry
    driver in Section 8:
    steer/near/clear/appear/rear/beer.
    Still pictures from the film may be used to remind the
    viewers of the contexts. .
    Close-up of Presenter's mouth as he forms the diphthong,
    and asks the viewers to repeat the words after him. The
    pictures may be shown again in a different order for the
    viewers to respond with the correct word.

11. *Reading*
(a) The policeman presents his report of the accident. This rolls
    from the bottom to the top of the screen at a predetermined
    speed. It may be typed or handwritten. The viewers are told
    to read it carefully, because they will have to answer questions
    about the report afterwards.
(b) Multiple choice answers are presented in written form for
    each question, which may be presented verbally or in writing.
    The questions are aimed at testing the viewers' memory and
    understanding of the information contained in the report.
    They are asked to select the correct choice of answer by
    saying its number.

12. *Listening*. The town planner talks about future changes in
    the design of towns. He refers to photographs, artists' draw-
    ings, filmed sequences. He speaks of the necessity for large car
    parks, for allowing less traffic into the centre of towns where
    people move about among shops and offices, and for restricting
    the activities of lorries to times when few people are about.
    The following patterns are written into the script:
    Plan A is more expensive than Plan B
    Plan B is not so expensive as Plan A
    Plan B is less expensive than Plan A
    Plan B is cheaper than Plan A.

Other examples which may be incorporated:
    More difficult/not so difficult/less difficult/easier
    more beautiful/not so beautiful/less beautiful/uglier
    more dangerous/not so dangerous/less dangerous/safer

13. *Writing.* The Presenter refers the viewers to their textbook, where a summary of the town planner's comments is set out. It contains blank spaces for the viewers to fill in with one of the transformations used above.
    Example:
    Loading is more difficult than unloading
    (Unloading is .... as/than loading)
    Crowded streets are more dangerous than empty streets
    (Empty streets are .... as/than crowded streets)
    The Presenter can be seen to fill in the first one or two blanks in a copy of the textbook as examples.

14. Traffic film to end the programme.

COMMENTS

This format provides flexibility within a unified theme. Each section may be extended or curtailed, depending upon the balance maintained between television and textbook. Each section contrasts with the preceding and succeeding section with regard to the type of activity required of the viewer. Since he is unsupervised, there is no guarantee that he will respond when asked to do so. His response is therefore restricted, except in Sections 5 and 7. Even if he is not prepared to say the required sentences out loud, he will, perhaps, make the transformation sub-vocally.

Such a format provides a good deal of incidental teaching, in the opportunities it gives for using aerial photographs, street models and plans, charts and diagrams of all kinds. These media involve conventions which need to be understood; they may require particular treatment to enable an audience to become familiar with them. The same point applies to the television conventions employed. If the audience is used to watching television, they will accept rapid jumps in location. A feature such as Section 9 could be split up into a number of very short sequences and interspersed throughout the programme, in order to hold attention. Such decisions will depend on how well the producer knows his audience.

FORMAT THREE
SITUATION

(a) This programme is aimed at the upper level of secondary education, in a country where English is a second language, and is a medium of instruction in secondary schools. The students are supervised by trained teachers of English.

(b) There is a lacuna between the activities of the English class and the activities of other subject areas; each assumes that the other is responsible for handling the particular English language requirements of geography, maths or science. A television series is designed to fill this gap.

(c) Language teaching at the levels of phonology and structure are dealt with by the English teacher; television only handles the forms of language in so far as they relate to the demands of the specific subject area. In addition, television is asked to supply stimulus material for related activities, such as note-taking, report writing, the arrangement of ideas in a sequence, meaning relationships, and so on. The programmes are not based upon the textbooks used in the classroom, but full ancillary notes are provided to indicate how the programmes fit into the classroom syllabus.

(d) This programme plan is intended for students of physics. It takes Faraday as its theme, since this places the students' laboratory activities in an historical perspective, and relates their own experiments to their broader application. It concentrates on the use of the passive in writing up experiments.

SETTING

A Presenter could be used to link the sections of the programme plan, though it is not necessary—this depends upon the students' familiarity with television conventions. Three or four small acting areas are required, including space to demonstrate bench work in a laboratory. Actors may be employed to play Oersted, Faraday

and Davy, though this may be avoided by only showing hands
and coat sleeves of a Presenter during the experiments.

PROGRAMME PLAN

1. *Listening.* Film or photographic stills relating domestic uses
   of electricity to an electrical power generating station; show
   the generator itself which needs to be kept turning at a
   uniform speed by some means of mechanical energy—coal,
   oil, falling water, or nuclear fission. One type of power being
   converted into another.
   Mix to picture of Hans Christian Oersted. Mix to studio
   bench where his experiment is set up, with a wire carrying
   current, and a magnetic needle on a pivot. (Commentary
   to this sequence should be minimal, and should use only
   simple structures; students' familiarity with such words as
   'energy', 'generator', will be known by reference to their
   physics textbook.)

2. *Listening and Reading.* Oersted describes his experiment as
   he does it. After each stage, he writes in his notebook. His
   spoken sentences are active, his written sentences passive.
   They are shown to the viewers as handwriting. They may
   or may not be read aloud by the viewers.

   Examples:
   Says: 'Look, I place the wire parallel to the magnetic
              needle. And the needle has moved.'
   Writes: When the wire is placed parallel to the magnetic
              needle, the needle is deflected.
   Says: 'And now I'll position the wire at right angles
              to the needle. But this time the needle doesn't
              move.'
   Writes: When the wire is positioned at right angles to
              the needle, it is not deflected.

   Later, he places the wire above and below the needle, and
   changes the direction of the current in the wire, and notes
   the direction of the needle's deflection.

3. *Speaking.* Show the sentence: 'A current *was passed* through the wire'. Explain the use of the passive in descriptions of experiments. Show a series of pictures illustrating various experiments; say the active sentence. Viewers must produce the verbal transformation to the passive.

Examples:
　　Two wires were attached to the battery.
　　The liquid was poured into the jar.
　　The magnet was fastened to a copper rod.
　　The mercury in the tube was measured.

Examples should be taken from experiments known to the students (Physics lesson); the variety of passive forms employed—singular, plural, past, present, future—will depend upon their familiarity with the structure (English lesson).

4. *Listening.* Faraday in his laboratory. He relates Oersted's experiment to his own, and demonstrates his apparatus. Two bowls of mercury, one with a fixed magnet and a free-moving wire; the other with a fixed wire and a movable magnet. When the circuit is completed to a battery, the magnet and the wire begin to rotate.

5. *Reading*

(a) A description of the apparatus and a report of the experiment is printed out on a roller caption. Since the material is fairly detailed, it is rolled from the bottom to the top of the screen at a slow rate. The description incorporates the passive patterns practised in Section 3. The viewers are told to read carefully, since they will be asked questions about the passage afterwards.

(b) A labelled diagram of the apparatus is available to the students either in notes provided for them, or drawn by the teacher on the blackboard. The diagram serves as a reference for the questions which follow. The questions are printed out on the screen, together with a choice of possible answers. Students may either read the correct answer or call out the number of the correct answer. Questions may elicit information, the correct passive form (blank-filling), or an interpretation of the data presented (the function of the mercury, for example).

Note: Response to questions in Sections 3 and 5 may be left to the control of the teacher, who can point to individuals in the class to answer each time.

6. *Listening.* A sequence on film or photographic stills, relating Faraday's experiment to modern uses of the electric motor. The point is made that electricity is being used to make mechanical power. Again, the commentary is short and simple.

7. *Meaning.* Sets of pictures or film-clips are shown, and viewers are asked to say what each set has in common—how they might classify them. Present two sample sets first.

Examples:
   mill-wheel/motor car/crane/wrist-watch (mechanical power)
   lamp/hair-dryer/door bell/electric stove (electrical power)
   radio/record-player/door-bell/telephone (electricity to produce sound)
   vacuum cleaner/washing machine/record-player/film-projector (electric motor)

This is not a right/wrong exercise; it encourages students to make connections. Discuss each set after it has been shown.

8. *Listening.* A picture of Sir Humphry Davy. Explain that Faraday was accused of stealing his ideas from another scientist, and that Davy attacked him in a very *sarcastic* speech. Sarcasm is to say one thing while you mean something quite different. An actor may speak the words, or they may be heard to the accompaniment of contemporary prints.

Example:
   'I say that Mr Faraday is very clever, for he can hear, run and write better than any man I know. Having heard

of the electrical experiments of Dr. Wollaston, he ran home to try them himself. He can run very quickly! Having completed the experiments, he wrote them down. He can write very quickly! Having written them down, he presents them as his own ideas. This is, indeed, the work of a great scientist!'

9. *Speaking.* Faraday introduces his famous iron-ring experiment, which is shown in five still photographs or drawings.

(a) Two coils of wire were wound on either side of an iron ring.
(b) One coil was connected to a galvanometer.
(c) The other coil was joined to a battery.
(d) When the battery was joined, it caused deflection on the galvanometer.
(e) When the connection was broken, it caused deflection in the other direction.

Viewers are asked to repeat the sequence of events. Each picture is shown, with key words or phrases superimposed as a guide:

(a) were wound
(b) was connected
(c) was joined
(d) When the battery was joined
(e) When the connection was broken . . .

The classroom teacher is asked to select individual students to supply each sentence.

10. *Note-taking.* Students are referred to their notebooks, where space is provided for them to take notes. There are six lines —one for each stage of the description—and certain words are already written in as guides.

Faraday continues to the development from his iron-ring experiment:

(a) The two *circuits* of wire were wound round a pasteboard *cylinder*.
(b) The *ends* were attached to a *galvanometer* and a battery.

(c) A magnet was *pushed* into the cylinder and *caused* deflection.

(d) When it was *taken out*, it caused deflection in the *other* direction.

(e) When it remained in the coil, *nothing* happened.

(f) Electricity was *induced* in the second coil by the movement of the magnet.

The italicized words are those written in the student's book. The presentation should be at normal speed, not leaving sufficient time for the students to write down everything.

However, the sequence may be repeated—again at normal speed. At the end of this section, a sample set of notes for the six stages may be shown and discussed.

11. *Listening.* A sequence on film or photographic stills, relating Faraday's experiment to the modern electric generator. Illustrate how the movement of his hand, in moving the magnet which causes the induced current, is today reproduced by mechanical energy, which can maintain continuous movement.

12. *Reading.* Faraday is shown with his *Experimental Researches in Electricity*. He introduces the following passage, which viewers are asked to read:

> A large copper disc was mounted on an axle between two poles of a magnet. Rubbing contacts were applied to the axle and the circumference of the disc. The wires were connected to a galvanometer. The disc was then rotated, and the galvanometer needle was permanently deflected. Thus a continuous current was shown to exist in the circuit.

(This passage is printed on a roller caption.)

13. *Writing.* Students are referred to their notes, in which the above passage is set out in frames, together with two further reports. The students are asked to write out the passage they have just read, after the programme, and to write out the other two reports.

Example:

| A large copper disc | were placed |
| Two grams of sulphur | were wound |
Two coils of wire	was mounted
on a dish	between two poles of a magnet
on an axle	made of pasteboard
round a cylinder	over a flame

14. End the programme—film sequence of modern uses of electricity or photomontage, or studio shots of Faraday with one of his experiments.

COMMENTS

Such a format falls between two extremes which might be employed at the upper secondary level. On the one hand, it may be considered too detailed—a more general approach to Faraday as a man might be preferred; an evocation of the scientific interest of 1820–1 might be attempted, referring to the work of Davy, Faraday, Ampère, Arago, Oersted and others. On the other hand, a country in which there is a lack of laboratory equipment in schools may prefer to have a programme more directly connected to the physics syllabus. This will particularly apply where there are no facilities for physics lessons on TV. The disadvantage of the former plan is the difficulty of incorporating such features as note-taking, report writing, and the understanding of a logical sequence of spoken and written ideas. The disadvantage of the latter plan is the difficulty of combining language teaching with direct physics teaching, and making both parts effective. The compromise we have suggested combines general interest with opportunities for a number of language activities.

Some activities, such as spoken responses, are kept to a minimum, partly because of the nature of the subject-matter, and partly because secondary school students are less likely to respond willingly than are elementary school students. Material for the listening and reading skills is closely related to the type of material students will meet in their science lessons where they require these skills. It is assumed, however, that the teaching of structural patterns has been carried out by the English teacher. Section 10 provides practice in note-taking, and students will inevitably miss some of the information in the video channel while they are writing. They are taking notes, however, from the audio channel principally; the visual information—shots of the actual experiment—is not essential to the total message, at this particular point.

The format allows for the use of a wide range of visual material. Sections 1, 6 and 11 can employ animations, cutaways, and diagrams in addition to conventional film shots or stills. Again, something needs to be known about the conventions acceptable to the audience. This applies equally to links between sections; it may be thought necessary to use a Presenter, perhaps using the vernacular, to do this in the early programmes of a series.

In an English-medium secondary school system, all subjects have particular language problems. The format, here applied to physics, can be equally successful when based upon material from the other sciences, mathematics, social studies, physical education or the arts. Modern methods of teaching mathematics have a strong visual emphasis. The industrial applications of chemistry, or the social implications of biological and zoological studies can all provide material. The possible approaches are innumerable, but the task of selection has a clear rationale: the theme selected, though related to a particular area of study, is not intended to do anything but reinforce the study of that subject; the theme is primarily selected for the opportunities it gives for teaching and practising a range of language skills appropriate to the subject.

Further Reading

The subject of this book is inter-disciplinary. Ideally, the educational technologist has to be aware of the pedagogical implications of the specialist subject; he has to match these to his knowledge of the possibilities and limitations of the machine or medium. The job is made easier if each side knows something of the other's problems. The language teacher must know what television can and cannot do; the TV producer needs to know why the language teacher makes the demands he does. The following short bibliography, by no means comprehensive, is intended to make each side more comprehensible to the other.

1A Linguistics

Crystal, David *Linguistics* Penguin 1971
Halliday, M. A. K., McIntosh, A., and Strevens, P. *The Linguistic Sciences and Language Teaching* Longmans 1964
Lyons, J. *Chomsky* Fontana 1971
Lyons, J. (ed.) *New Horizons in Linguistics* Penguin 1970
Robins, R. H. *General Linguistics: An Introductory Survey* Longmans 1964

1B Language Teaching

Diack, Hunter *In spite of the Alphabet* Chatto & Windus 1965
Fraser, Hugh, and O'Donnell, W. R. (eds.) *Applied Linguistics and the Teaching of English* Longmans 1969
Fry, Edward *Teaching Faster Reading: A manual* Cambridge University Press 1963
Gray, W. S. *The Teaching of Reading and Writing* UNESCO 1965

Harding, David H. *The New Pattern of Language Teaching* Longmans 1967
Hickel, Raymond *Modern Language Teaching and Television* Council of Europe 1965
Mackey, William Francis *Language Teaching Analysis* Longmans 1965
Macmillan, M. *Efficiency in Reading* ETIC, the British Council 1965
Pit Corder, S. *English Language Teaching and Television* Longmans 1960
Pit Corder, S. *The Visual Element in Language Teaching* Longmans 1966
Rivers, Wilga M. *The Psychologist and the Foreign Language Teacher* Chicago University Press 1964
Rivers, Wilga M. *Teaching Foreign Language Skills* Chicago University Press 1968
Valdman, Albert (ed.) *Trends in Language Teaching* McGraw-Hill 1966

2A Educational Technology

Coppen, Helen *A Survey of British Research in Audio-Visual Aids* National Committee for Audio-Visual Aids in Education 1968
Emery, F. E. (ed.) *Systems Thinking: Selected Readings* Penguin 1969
Leedham, J., and Unwin, D. *Programmed Learning in the Schools* Longmans 1965
MacKenzie, Norman, Eraut, Michael, and Jones, Hywel C. *Teaching and Learning: an introduction to new methods and resources in higher education* UNESCO: IIEP 1970
McLuhan, Marshall *Understanding Media* Sphere Books 1967
Richmond, W. K. (ed.) *The Concept of Educational Technology* Weidenfeld & Nicolson 1970.
Schramm, W., Coombs, P. H., Kahnert, F., and Lyle, J. *The New Media: Memo to Educational Planners* UNESCO: IIEP 1967
Schramm, W. *Mass Media and National Development* Stanford University Press & UNESCO 1964

Taylor, L. C. *Resources for Learning* Penguin 1971

Trenaman, J. M. *Communication and Comprehension* Longmans 1967

2B   Educational Television

Chu, G. C., and Schramm, W. *Learning from Television: What the Research Says* National Association of Educational Broadcasters 1968

Gibson, T. *The Practice of ETV* Hutchinson Educational 1970

Gibson, T. *The Use of ETV* Hutchinson Educational 1970

Groombridge, Brian *Television and the People* Penguin 1972

Hancock, A. *Planning for ETV* Longmans 1971

Maclean, R. *Television in Education* Methuen 1968

Moir, G. (ed.) *Teaching and Television: ETV Explained* Pergamon 1967

Scupham, J. *Broadcasting and the Community* Watts 1967

Index